Loyalism and Labour in Belfast:
The Autobiography of Robert McElborough, 1884–1952

Edited by
Emmet O'Connor and Trevor Parkhill

CORK **cup** UNIVERSITY PRESS

First published in 2002 by
Cork University Press
Cork
Ireland

© Cork University Press 2002

British Library Cataloguing in Publication Data
A CIP catalogue record for this book is available from the British Library.
ISBN 1 85918 278 X

Typesetting by Red Barn Publishing, Skeagh, Skibbereen, Co. Cork
Printed in Ireland by ColourBooks, Baldoyle, Co. Dublin

www.corkuniversitypress.com

Loyalism and Labour in Belfast

The Autobiography of Robert McElborough,
1884–1952

IRISH NARRATIVES

IRISH NARRATIVES

Series edited by David Fitzpatrick

Personal narratives of past lives are essential for understanding any field of history. They provide unrivalled insight into the day-to-day consequences of political, social, economic or cultural relationships. Memoirs, diaries and personal letters, whether by public figures or obscure witnesses of historical events, will often captivate the general reader as well as engrossing the specialist. Yet the vast majority of such narratives are preserved only among the manuscripts or rarities in libraries and archives scattered over the globe. The aim of this series of brief yet scholarly editions is to make available a wide range of narratives concerning Ireland and the Irish over the last four centuries. All documents, or sets of documents, are edited and introduced by specialist scholars, who guide the reader through the world in which the text was created.

Other titles in the series:

Andrew Bryson's Ordeal: An Epilogue to the 1798 Rebellion, ed. by Michael Durey
Henry Stratford Persse's Letters from Galway to America, 1821–1832, ed. by James L. Pethica and James C. Roy
A Redemptorist Missionary in Ireland, 1851–1854: Memoirs by Joseph Prost, C.Ss.R. trans. and ed. by Emmet Larkin and Herman Freudenberger
Frank Henderson's Easter Rising: Recollections of a Dublin Volunteer, ed. by Michael Hopkinson
A Patriot Priest: The Life of Father James Coigly, 1761–1798, ed. by Dáire Keogh
'My Darling Danny': Letters from Mary O'Connell to Her Son Daniel, 1830–1832, ed. by Erin I. Bishop
The Rebel in his Family: Selected Papers of William Smith O'Brien, ed. by Richard and Marianne Davis
The Reynolds Letters: An Irish Emigrant Family in Late Victorian Manchester, ed. by Lawrence W. McBride
A Policeman's Ireland: Recollections of Samuel Waters, RIC, ed. by Stephen Ball
'The Misfit Soldier': Edward Casey's War Story, 1914–1918, ed. by Joanna Bourke
Alfred Webb: The Autobiography of a Quaker Nationalist, ed. by Marie-Louise Legg
Pádraig Ó Fathaigh's War of Independence: Recollections of a Galway Gaelic Leaguer, ed. by Timothy G. McMahon
An Englishwoman in Belfast: Rosamond Stephen's Record of the Great War, ed. by Oonagh Walsh
'As I was among the Captives': Joseph Campbell's Prison Diary, 1922–1923, ed. by Eiléan Ní Chuilleanáin

Forthcoming titles:

British Intelligence in Ireland, 1920–21: The Final Reports, ed. by Peter Hart
Scholar Bishop: The Recollections and Diary of Narcissus Marsh, 1693–96, ed. by Raymond Gillespie
A Viceroy's Vindication? Sir Henry Sidney's Memoir of Service in Ireland, 1556–78, ed. by Ciarán Brady

David Fitzpatrick teaches history at Trinity College, Dublin. His books include *Politics and Irish Life, 1913–1921* (1977, reissued 1998), *Oceans of Consolation: Personal Accounts of Irish Migration to Australia* (1995) and *The Two Irelands, 1912–1939* (1998).

Contents

Acknowledgements

The authors are grateful to a number of sources of assistance. Foremost among these is Peter Brooke who, when a research assistant in PRONI and encouraged by Dr Bill Crawford, made the diary accessible by his transcription. We are grateful to the Director of the Public Record Office of Northern Ireland for permission to reproduce extensive extracts, to Dr David Lammey, Head of Reader Services, for helpful advice and to the Search Room and Repository staff for their consistently courteous and efficient service. The Belfast City Council archivists, Robert Corbett, Joseph Heaney and Ian Montgomery, also provided useful information.

In this context, we are glad to record our thanks to the staffs in Belfast Central Library, Derry Central Library, The Linen Hall Library and to the University of Ulster library staff at the Coleraine and Magee College campuses.

We would also take this opportunity to acknowledge the interest and encouragement of friends, colleagues and former colleagues: Martyn Anglesea, Dr Bill Crawford, Kenneth Darwin, Francis Devine, Pauline Dickson, Robert Heslip, Jane Leonard, Dr Bill Maguire, John C. Nolan, Dr Vivienne Pollock, Dr Brian Trainor and Tom Wylie.

Introduction

The diary of Robert McElborough is in fact an autobiographical account written during the 1940s, when he had retired, of his experiences as an employee of two municipal services in Belfast—the tramways and the gas industry. Robert Henry McElborough was born on 11 February 1884 in Matilda Street[1]. He continued to live in this district of Sandy Row and Donegall Road throughout his life, save for a brief period in the early 1900s when, to be closer to his tram depot, he lived in Rockville Street in the heart of the Falls Road, an area he said was 'mixed' and where 'religion was never mentioned' [42].

The several references in the text to the 'new houses' to which he and his family moved, initially in Teutonic Street—'built with water closets, something new to the working class' [16]—then in Coolbeg Street and Coolfin Street, are reminders of the extent to which Belfast's burgeoning population was accommodated in inner-city new-build housing at a time when it was the fastest-growing city in the British Isles.[2] McElborough's parents had themselves been attracted to the city from their native county, Tyrone, probably in the early 1880s. His father, who initially had been a soldier, found work on the tramways where in turn Robert would work as a tram conductor and where, by 1907, he would first become associated with trade union activities. He intensified his involvement in trade union affairs when he left the trams to return to the gas industry just before the outbreak of the First World War, and here he continued to work until he was retired on health grounds in the early 1940s. When he died on 29 March 1952, his address was 10 Coolfin Street, still in the quarter where he had been born and raised.[3] The *Belfast & Ulster Directory* entry for this address records that a Mrs Margaret McElborough (who could have been Robert's second wife, his first wife having pre-deceased him) was resident there until 1972.

This account of his working life appears to have been prompted by McElborough's determination to keep a promise to Andrew Moore, a

friend and fellow trade unionist, that he would write a book with a view
to exposing the extent to which the interests of rank and file trade
union members in the General & Municipal Workers' Union had been
ignored by their union officials [65]. This is in fact his second version:
he had apparently given his first account to a fellow trade unionist who
had not returned it. His stated aim in this replacement version was 'to
do my best to recall the most important facts of my history in the Gas
Industry and Trade Union movement' [15]. From the dates given,
McElborough presumably embarked on his second version, which runs
to four manuscript volumes, sometime after February 1946.

In February 1949 McElborough wrote in response to a newspaper
item by John Hewitt, then Curator of Art in the Belfast Museum and
Art Gallery (which in 1962 became the Ulster Museum): 'I have been
raised in humble circumstances and very little education. I have done
my best to give the true facts of my life in the story I have written. Perhaps you could help me?' The McElborough archive, comprising the
diaries and associated correspondence between him and Hewitt, was
subsequently deposited in the Public Record Office of Northern Ireland in July 1956.[4] Its value as a source for trade union and labour history research first became evident in the transcripts compiled by Peter
Brooke of PRONI and issued in association with 'The People's Exhibition', an Ulster Museum display sponsored by the Irish Congress of
Trade Unions in 1974.[5]

McElborough's autobiography is of intrinsic interest as a rare
account of a worker's life, told by a witness to some of the leading
events in Belfast labour history between 1907 and 1945. McElborough
is not strong on factual history. The narrative is frequently anachronis-
tic, out of sequence, bitterly subjective, or based on a conflation of
myth and memory. Though footnoted in most recent histories of con-
temporaneous Belfast labour, it is of limited use as a source for organi-
zational research. However, as Irish labour historiography progresses
beyond fact-gathering to studies of mentalities, personal and popular
memory, and relations within the workplace and within trade unions,
it will find the memoir to have a greater value.

Some themes in the text are obvious and easily appreciated: the sheer inhumanity of the working conditions, the fear of a family man reluctantly defying the anti-trade unionism of his workplace supervisors, the frustration of discharging thankless union duties, and the 'workerist' attitude to union officialdom. A covert theme is what might be called Protestant labourism. With the growth of British-based unions in Ireland in the late nineteenth century, British labour values were superimposed on a mainly Protestant membership in Ulster. Increasingly, trade union leaders emerged from those few who felt comfortable with a secular, class-oriented movement, in communion with Britain but in affiliation with the Irish Trade Union Congress in Dublin, supportive of Labour politics, and anti-Unionist if not necessarily against the Union.

McElborough's is a voice of the silent majority who were sidelined in this process. In Sandy Row, Linfield mill, the Corporation, and the shipyards, he lived and worked within an overwhelmingly Protestant environment.[6] The two unions he belonged to were noted also for their loyalist proclivities. McElborough writes as one 'proud to state that I . . . fought on the workers' side for wages and conditions as a descendant of an Ulster Scot' [54]. He disliked coming under the authority of English trade union officials, and welcomed the formation of a breakaway Ulster union in the 1940s. The political dimension to this is alluded to obliquely in the comparison between Alex Boyd and his successors, his unease about supporting Labour politics in the 1920s, and the repeated criticism of Englishmen opining on the Irish question [35,42]. There is no doubt that McElborough was an *Ulster* Unionist.

McElborough also illustrates the potential and limits of Protestant labourism. His politics were compatible with trade union militancy, and open to some vague accommodation with nationalists [42]. Apart from a malign view of the political influence of the Catholic Church, there is no trace of sectarianism in the memoir [42]. McElborough had Catholic friends and enjoyed Irish music 'sessions' in MacEntee's pub in King Street [45]. At the same time, his apparent blindness towards sectarianism extended to discounting it as a political and economic problem. He simply has nothing to say on Belfast's working class divisions whereas, in theory at least, British labour offered the solution of incorporation within a wider, secular, trade union movement.

McElborough first expressed his politics within the unlikely setting of the Ulster Liberal Association [40–42]. The conditions for this unique conjuncture might be traced to 1902, when the Unionist Party lost a Westminster by-election in South Belfast to Tom Sloan, a semi-skilled shipyard worker, nominated by the Belfast Protestant Association. Standing for 'Protestantism, Orangeism, total abstinence [and] trade unionism', Sloan held the seat until 1910.[7] In 1903, Sloan founded the Independent Orange Order [100], and Sandy Row was its heartland, with sixteen lodges in 1907. During the 1906 general election, 'the great majority of windows in those streets [around Sandy Row and Donegall Road] displayed portraits of Mr Sloan. . .'.[8] McElborough does not refer to Sloan, but he campaigned in elections for Alex Boyd, secretary of the Municipal Employees' Association (MEA), a prominent Independent Orangeman, a Sloanite, and a city councillor for St George's ward [35]. He was familiar too with the oratory of the Belfast Protestant Association's leader, Arthur Trew; all Belfast knew of Trew, a regular Sunday afternoon demagogue on the Custom House steps, Belfast's Speakers' Corner [46].

While Sloan remained a loyalist, the IOO's Imperial Grand Master, Robert Lindsay Crawford, was edging towards liberalism. In 1905, Crawford persuaded the IOO to endorse the 'Magheramorne manifesto', which appealed for a constructive Irish patriotism in place of political division and sectarianism. Belfast Liberals were meanwhile cultivating the IOO. In the 1906 general election, seven candidates ran on the same platform as T.W. Russell, MP for South Tyrone, a Liberal Unionist of some radical views, and subsequently a Home Ruler. Several 'Russellites' were associated with the IOO, and later joined the Liberals. Following the Liberal landslide in the elections, the Ulster Liberal Association was born in April, and from January 1907, Crawford edited the Association's paper, the *Ulster Guardian*. Impressed by the big dockers' and carters' strike in the summer of 1907, Crawford tried to infuse the *Guardian* with a labourist stance on social issues, and it was this coverage which convinced McElborough to join the Liberals [40–42].

Despite the long established Liberal-Labour, or 'Lib-Lab', tradition in Britain, neither Crawford nor McElborough had much luck in trying to link the Belfast Liberals with trade unionism. Crawford was compelled to resign as editor of the *Ulster Guardian* by the board of the paper in 1908. McElborough stayed on, relishing the Liberal Association's pluralism on constitutional politics. It would seem that, as with so many Irish socialists, the thing that animated him most was the national question. His breaking point with the Liberals was over an incident during the third Home Rule crisis: their invitation to Winston Churchill in February 1912 [42]. Churchill defended the government's Home Rule policy in Celtic Park with Ulster Liberal leader Lord Pirrie and Nationalists. The rally aroused intense Unionist indignation, which prevented it from taking place in the Ulster Hall. McElborough's subsequent political activism was confined to municipal elections in the 1920s, when he championed Alex Boyd, still a loyalist but returned as an Independent Labour alderman for St Anne's in 1920 and St George's in 1924,[9] and campaigned more reluctantly for his union secretary, Sam Bradley [58].

McElborough's trade union involvement began in November 1907, when he joined the Municipal Employees' Association [22]. The Belfast Municipal Employees' and Other Workers' Society was registered in 1896, and reported a membership of 418 in 1903, and 600 in 1904.[10] Alexander Bowman was its first secretary, and he was succeeded by Alex Boyd in 1901.[11] In 1905 it merged into the British MEA. Before the 1890s, trade unionism was confined largely to artisans, and the MEA was a reflex of 'new unionism', a movement to organize general and semi-skilled sectors. As McElborough shows, it was grudgingly tolerated by the Corporation before 1914. The long working week—over seventy-two hours—on the trams caused him to 'interview' Boyd about membership. The choice of Boyd is significant, as the Tyneside-based National Amalgamated Union of Labour was also organizing

tramwaymen, and pursuing a more militant line than the MEA, to no
great effect. McElborough may also have been inspired by the 1907
dockers' and carters' strike, led by Jim Larkin, which had an enormous
impact on the city.[12] McElborough recollects his colleagues' discussion
of it, the watchfulness of the inspectors, and Boyd's leading role in the
fight, but is confused on some details [29]. He recalls the dispute as
occurring around 1913, the year Larkin fought the famous lock-out in
Dublin, and as culminating in victory rather than a barely mitigated
defeat. He also associates Ben Tillet with the dockers' eventual recovery. Tillet led a London-based dockers' union, whereas Belfast's dockers belonged to the Liverpool-based National Union of Dock Labourers
in 1907. The (Catholic) deep-sea section then defected to Larkin's Irish
Transport and General Workers' Union on its formation in 1909. Boyd
was instrumental in persuading the (Protestant) cross-channel men not
to join the Transport Union.[13]

Boyd's loss of his Council seat in 1907 made the MEA more vulner-
able to Corporation hostility. He may have further weakened his base
when he left the IOO that same year, saying it had nothing to offer the
working class. The branch declined, and Boyd ceased to be secretary in
1912.[14] His successors are unclear. The 'organizer from Glasgow' was
probably A. R. Turner, who represented the MEA at the 1914 Irish
Trade Union Congress; Denis Houston was from Donegal [30].[15] The
MEA's debility is evident from its reliance on activists outside the union
such as Houston, and 'D. Gordon', probably Dawson Gordon, secretary of the Flaxroughers' Union. Alex Bowman had also combined
posts in the MEA and the Flaxroughers.

A general trade union recovery materialized during the later war
period, and the brief economic boom that followed. These were years
of major industrial unrest, and the memoir notes various disputes and
a strike of municipal employees [38–40]. Contemporary government
records, which are not exhaustive on Ireland, logged two pertinent
strikes in Belfast in 1918: one of 289 gasworks labourers for a wage
increase which lasted from 9 to 11 May, and was unsuccessful; and the
other of 433 municipal employees and contractors' carters from 30

September to 12 November.[16] This second strike, probably that recalled by McElborough, was over conditions, and ended in compromise. The biggest conflict of the period was the unofficial strike of 30,000 engineering and shipbuilding workers for a forty-four-hour week on 25 January 1919.[17] The dispute extended to municipal employees, leaving Belfast without gas or electricity for three weeks, and McElborough confronting hardship and personal animosity [38–39]. Dublin Castle regarded the unrest as symptomatic of 'Bolshevism', and sent in the army on 15 February to take over the gasworks and power station. Within ten days the strike had collapsed.

In July 1920, Belfast was on the verge of a slump, and two years of lethal sectarian disturbances. On 21 July, the Belfast Protestant Association instigated workplace expulsions in the shipyards, and the terror spread spontaneously. To protect loyal Protestant employment, smash socialism within the labour movement, and create a more homogeneous Northern Ireland, at least 7,400 people were driven from their jobs by the end of the year. With a mainly Protestant, left-wing, anti-partitionist leadership, trade unions were a prime target of loyalist suspicion. One quarter of recorded expelled workers were Protestants. 'Every man who was prominently known in the labour movement, who was known as an [Independent Labour Party member] was expelled from his work just the same as the rebel Sinn Feiners', Labour Councillor James Baird told the British Trades Union Congress in 1920.[18] Vigilance committees were set up to confirm the new realities on the shopfloor, their leaders drawn from the Unionist Party's Ulster Unionist Labour Association. It is possibly one of these committees to which McElborough refers in noting that 'there were a lot of secret meetings being held and a vigilant committee had been formed for the purpose of appointing a foreman to replace Gordon with a loyalist' [31]. As a member of the Independent Labour Party, the Irish Trade Union Congress executive, and an anti-partitionist, Gordon was the classic 'rotten Prod'. McElborough makes no judgment on the expulsions, though Boyd offered the conventional defences, claiming variously that the victims were Sinn Féiners, that trade unionism had been manipulated by

Sinn Féin and socialists, and that men from the south and west had taken the jobs 'of those brave lads who went to the front' during the war.[19] The political disturbances which followed the expulsions had left 455 dead and over 2,000 wounded by June 1922.[20] McElborough provides a pitiful account of his superiors' indifference to the dangers he faced in keeping the street lamps lit amidst the terror [47–49].

The slump injected an urgency into British trade unionism's post-war merger mania. In 1924 the MEA combined with the National Amalgamated Union of Labour (NAUL) and the National Union of General Workers to form the National Union of General and Municipal Workers (NUGMW).[21] It seemed to McElborough as if the MEA was being merged with the NAUL, as only these unions had branches in Belfast, the NAUL having organized semi-skilled men in the shipyards since 1890, and competed with the MEA on the trams in the 1900s [56–57]. McElborough found less cause for animus against the third union involved, which supplied the NUGMW's secretary, Will Thorne.

Thorne was a legendary hero of 'new unionism', and, by the 1920s, a veteran MP and elder statesman of the movement in the twilight of his union career.[22] His background, renown, and easy manner evidently charmed the curmudgeonly Belfastman. The narrative draws heavily on versions of the Thorne legend which were presumably retailed among Belfast tram and gasworkers; though, in best Belfast tradition, McElborough's anecdotes cut the hero down to size [36]. Thorne was a stoker in London's giant Beckton gasworks in 1889 when he founded the National Union of Gasworkers and General Labourers (from 1916 the National Union of General Workers). Within months he had recruited 20,000 members, and forced the gas companies to slash the working day from twelve to eight hours. Later that year he led a celebrated attack on strike-breakers in Leeds. The Gasworkers' Union began organizing in Belfast in late 1889, and secured a wage increase and the eight-hour day from the Corporation. In June 1890, it extended recruitment to tramwaymen. The Gasworkers' Union had eight branches in Belfast by 1892, but, as with most of the 'new unions', its Irish sections had collapsed by 1895.[23] The MEA was a separate union, and there is no reason why Thorne should have had contact with Belfast members before 1924. McElborough transposes events of 1889–93, of which he may have heard as a boy, to the early 1920s, and imagines that he was there himself.

The 'green sash' incident is fairly well known in Belfast trade union folklore. It occurred in 1893, when the city hosted the British Trades Union Congress. To mark the end of the Congress, the trades' council organized a parade on Sunday 9 September, culminating in a rally in Ormeau Park. The House of Lords had rejected Gladstone's second Home Rule Bill that Friday, and the British delegates—most of whom were sympathetic to Home Rule—were advised to be discreet. Thorne would have appreciated the situation. Born in Birmingham of Irish parents, he remembered Catholic-Protestant rioting as a child. At the same time he did not hold deep feelings on Ireland. While favouring Home Rule, he was not an Irish nationalist. The sash he wore in Ormeau Park waiting for the speeches to begin sported his union's colours of red, white, and green. After some argument, he was persuaded to remove it before ascending the platform because 'there's too much green in it'.[24] In any case, the meeting was soon broken up by an organized anti-Home Rule clique, causing some rising stars of the most powerful trade union movement in the world to flee in disarray. A common rendition of the affair, intended to illustrate the paranoia of loyalists *per se*, is that Thorne had provoked a spontaneous riot by appearing on the platform with a green sash. McElborough's twist, related in such exceptional fluency that it may have been a popular Protestant version, turns it into a joke about English naïvety. A final myth about Thorne, cited by McElborough, is that he was illiterate. Legend has it that he was taught to read and write by Eleanor Marx; which is almost true. According to Thorne's very readable autobiography, Eleanor 'used to assist me to improve my reading and handwriting, which was very bad at the time'.[25]

McElborough's appraisal of the 1924 merger and its consequences is subjective, though not without foundation. The MEA had been a small union by British standards, beset by chronic problems because its rivals resented its policy of advancement through Labour politics rather than industrial militancy. In a cynical manoeuvre the TUC and Labour Party ruled, in 1908, that exclusive public service trade unionism was divisive, compelling the MEA to disaffiliate or have its members handed over to other unions.[26] To alleviate its subsequent near-ostracization, the MEA allied with the Workers' Union and the NAUL in 1919, creating an umbrella body, the National Amalgamated Workers' Union. However, each leg of the tripos retained separate bargaining structures, and the alliance collapsed in 1921–2.[27] These were difficult years for the MEA, whose membership dropped from 65,000 in 1920 to 41,000 in 1923.[28] In the ultimate merger, it constituted the smallest element of the NUGMW. Overnight, McElborough moved from a select fraternity to Britain's second biggest general union, with 360,000 members, and its Belfast base chiefly in the shipyards.

McElborough resented the shipyard men, who suffered severe unemployment during the inter-war years, as a drain on resources, and it is true that while the MEA was financially secure in 1924, the NAUL was virtually bankrupt [56].[29] Some of his other complaints have a validity [57]. The MEA had few paid officials, and a decentralized, horizontal structure, whereas the NUGMW concentrated power in District Secretaries, who acquired a reputation for nepotism, and managing union elections through machine politics.[30] The post of Irish District Secretary went to Sam Bradley, an official of the NAUL since 1919. Further centralization took place under Charles Dukes, who replaced the elderly Thorne as General Secretary in 1934. As McElborough observes, Dukes had lost his youthful radicalism and was wary of his members. Whatever he thought about McElborough 'carrying a revolver' [57], he suspected rank and file movements as Communist inspired.[31] Dukes restructured his jaded administration in 1937. Bradley retired, and the loss-making Irish district, the smallest in the union with 6,000 members, was merged with Liverpool and North Wales under the Liverpool-based District Officer Andrew Basnett.[32]

McElborough's last trade union initiative was to encourage the Ulster Transport and Allied Operatives' Union (UTAOU), which he welcomed as an assertion of local rank-and-file democracy. Formed around 1945 by busmen unhappy with the Amalgamated Transport and General Workers' Union, the UTAOU expanded to 8,000 members by 1954, most of them in public transport. As a splinter body, with a reputation for poaching, it was regarded with some suspicion by the Northern Ireland Committee of the Irish Trade Union Congress. It was also one of the few unions to resist the Committee's efforts to promote affiliation to the Dublin-based Congress in the immediate post-war period. McElborough's account possibly confuses the UTAOU story with another poaching wrangle involving NUGMW gasworkers and the Amalgamated Transport and General Workers' Union.[33] At any rate, the UTAOU emerged from the Amalgamated Transport and General Workers' Union and eventually merged with the NUGMW![34]

The UTAOU was the last hurrah of Ulster trade unionism outside the public service. Today, predominantly British-based trade unions boast that they have maintained a united, secular movement in a divided society. In respect of organization at least, it is a proud and justified claim and, given the horrors of 1920, one not lightly dismissed. Yet the efficient secret, and the secret inefficacy, of Northern Ireland trade unionism lies in mass non-active participation in the movement, and its domination by a self-selecting elite committed to labourist values at odds with those of their members. No doubt Robert McElborough would have had something to say about that.

Editorial Note

Robert McElborough's four-volume autobiography was written with a hasty fluency, perhaps because he had already written one version (which he had given to a trade union colleague who had not returned it). Full stops have been added where they have contributed to an understanding of the sense of the diary. Words have been inserted in square brackets with the same purpose. In the Introduction, citations to the appropriate page of the narrative are given in square brackets. To make clear the distinction between trade unions, unionism and unionists, an upper case U is used for the Union with Britain, and for political Unionism or Unionists, whether members of the Unionist Party or not. Since McElborough's narrative does not follow a simple chronological sequence, dates have been inserted at various points to ease the reader's task.

Autobiography of Robert McElborough

[PRONI, D/770/1/1–4]

In re-writing my life story, I might not be able to give the same facts which I wrote in my original manuscript which I spent over two years in writing, and which I gave to an ex-Trade Union official on request to review and correct before publication. I have waited since Xmas 1944 until Feb. 1946. Between these dates I have enquired the reason for the delay but the replies to my queries have convinced [me] that I will have to wait some considerable time (if ever) before I receive my manuscript back again, hence my second attempt so I will do my best to recall the most important facts of my history in the Gas Industry and the Trade Union movement in my young days up to the present.[1]

I was born in 13 Matilda St. on the 11.2.1884. My father who had been in the Hussars for the period he had enlisted, came to Belfast from Tyrone. His knowledge of horses was an asset when he applied to the Belfast City Tramways for a job. Mr A. Nance who engaged him placed him in charge of the tram track. His duties were to keep the track sanded on frosty weather and to water the rail in dry weather. To do this work he had six horses under his control. He had no regulated hours, he was always on duty. If he was taking a meal at home it was mostly a hurried one. I never remember seeing my father at home at night but I remember my mother getting up in the morning after 4 to put sticks below the kettle to get my father a cup of soup before going to the tram depot, and sometimes if there was a heavy frost my father would be out all night putting salt on the track. He never to my knowledge had a day off. I never heard him making any complaint. Mr Nance was to him and the rest of the tram employees something far above them in the social scale. If he had asked them to go through hell they would have went if they knew the way.[2]

I was one of a family of thirteen[3], and after I had spent a few years in Matilda Street we removed to 24 Gaffikin Street, I suppose to get close to the tram depot and to his work. It was during the time we lived here that I spent my time amongst the horses and the strappers who looked after the horses who were taken to Shaftesbury Square to be changed. I spent my happy years until I reached the age of seven [1891] when my father got me engaged as a point-shifter. My elder brother had been taken on as a trace-boy. Ma Black's pub in Gaffikin Street was the local for tram men. There was a large room at the back with a fire and tram men finishing at night were admitted even after closing time which was 11 p.m. I collected many pennies from the tram men and I used to be scared when I heard a tram man who had taken one over the eight cursing the manager because he had received a sentence from Nance for something he had done during his work hours. When I told my mother she used to tell me not to repeat it as the man was drunk.

We moved from Gaffikin to Teutonic Street which was being built with water closets, something new to the working class, and it was during the time I was living there that the education act was passed.[4] Up to this children were free to attend school or stay away. This act meant that my job as a point shifter was finished. I had made up my mind with other boys not to go as we had been told how masters used the cane for punishment. My father who could not read or write selected the Blackstaff National School, Ennis Place, for me and the night before a number of us agreed to meet in the Bog Meadows instead. We carried out our intentions but each day our numbers dwindled until I and another boy were the only two left. I was always in bed every night when my father finished work but the School Inspector stopped my career of freedom. When I arrived home one evening he was waiting for me and the threat of telling my father if I did not enrol the following day was sufficient.

The master of this school put fear into every scholar. We were all boys and he certainly taught us. I remember pleading with my mother to allow me to stay at home on one occasion. She went out as I thought to do her shopping but she arrived back with the master. I felt the weight of his cane when I got to school. He would make the strongest boy carry the defaulter on his back whilst he followed up with the cane.

Scholars were compelled to bring a large piece of coal every Monday morning for the purpose of warming the school during the week. The master had to see each piece before you placed it with the rest. If it was a small piece you were sent back home for a larger piece. Many plans were adopted to get a larger piece. A boy would follow a bellman [coalman] until he stopped at a house to deliver a bag. As soon as he entered the house with his bag of coal the boy jumped the cart or van and exchanged his small piece of coal for a larger one.

I was not very long attending school when my father left his work. A messenger had called at my home with instructions to my father to go to Castle Junction with regard to some special car. There were no telephones then. My father after having his breakfast had went to the barbers to get shaved and afterwards went on to the tramway depot. The messenger when told my father had gone told my mother to tell my father if he returned. Afterwards when it was discovered that my father was attending to his horses in the depot, the manager told him he had ignored his instructions. When my father tried to explain, the manager would not listen and my father walked out. The next day, the manager, after getting the facts of the case, sent an inspector to tell him to return to work but my father had got his back up and refused to return. This meant curtains for us.

My mother before her marriage was a companion to two ladies who belong to Tyrone. She was educated and knew her Bible from cover to cover. Her daily routine was cooking on a coal fire, washing, baking and mending our clothes. When I came home after 11 at night, my mother would be engaged on some of these tasks. The mothers of this period were slaves in every sense of the word, and when my father made this decision I suppose he was of the opinion that he would get work else-where with his knowledge of horses. He attended carriers' stables each morning on the chance of some carter sleeping in. He got an odd day's work in this manner and he would return at night with the 2/6 [two shillings and sixpence] he earned for a day's pay. About twice a week this would happen and some weeks nothing. My mother had to sell or pawn articles of clothing or furniture to keep us from want, but this supply soon stopped and we had to remove to rooms in Matilda St. My experience of living in rooms with nothing to eat, only what friends gave us, is engraved on my memory. The pluck of my mother and her cheerful spirit, and her faith in God, were magnificent. We were put to bed on empty stomachs and my mother sang hymns to us until we fell asleep. My father went out in the morning and did not return until night. He did not I suppose tell anyone about the state of affairs at home. On some occasions he brought food home. But my mother's faith in God was justified when a lady came to inquire about my mother.

To me this lady is an angel for it was the finish of our poverty. My father got a job with a contractor and my elder brother got work. We moved into new houses that were being built in Coolbeg Street. Most of my school pals had got work in the machine room in Linfield mill on half-time.[5] I pleaded with my mother to let me go to work in the mill on half time. I was afraid of returning to our former position of living in rooms and hunger. My mother consented when I brought one of my pals who was on half time to tell her that we attended school every other day and his wages were 3/- [three shillings] weekly. I interviewed the machine master, who told me to get my birth certificate and bring it to the machine room at 6 am.

The morning I presented myself for work was a surprise. My pal had told me all about the machine and how you screw the flax into the holder, but when the machines started to go, I was scared at the noise they created. I was sent to what was called the coarse end of the machine to learn. It was some time before I could understand what the trainee was saying owing to the din of the machines. The hours were from 6 till 6, with ¾ [of an hour] for breakfast and an hour for dinner. The pouse and the tow were hanging about you and I believe I must have drunk quarts of water which was kept in a bucket with a lid on.[6] There are two at each end of the machine, and the trainee was giving me spells of screwing. In the afternoon, he left me with instructions to the boy beside to help me.

My first day in the machine [room] is unforgettable. The centre of my hand had a blister caused by the wrench when I tightened the nut each time on the holder. When I went to bed on my first day in the machine room, I was still at the machine with the holders falling on me. My mother came into my room a number of times during the night to quiet my nerves. This was my first encounter where the machine controls the worker. I was only nine at this time and I was glad when my mother allowed me to sleep the following morning until 9. The mill school was owned and controlled by the directors. We were taught the three Rs and had no coal to bring to school. There were two sets of boys in this school and no girls (our teachers were women), and the one set of boys challenged the other set to a football match on a Saturday evening in the plantation behind the mill, which is now Blythe Street. The rules for this match were: each player put up a penny, and to be played in our bare feet with a sixpenny ball, the winners to take the pool. We looked forward to this match every week.

Your pocket money was three pence weekly out of your weekly wage of 3/−. If you were promoted to the other end of the machine, your wages were increased by 3 pence. You paid your weekly visit to McCormick's Show in McTier Street. Admission to front seats a form [bench] 1d; your other penny was for black lumps. McCormick and his wife gave you a great show for the money. If my uncle came on a visit from Tyrone, I would receive before his time for returning a sixpence, which I invested in the Theatre Royal to see the lights of London or some Shakespeare play.[7] The rest of the boys used to envy me when I told them about the different plays I had seen.

I had almost reached the age of 13 [1897] when my hand got caught one Saturday morning when I was cleaning the machine with a hand brush whilst the machine was working. My hand was laid open and I was taken to the Frederick Street Hospital. I still have the scar where the stitches were.

This finished my career in the machine room, and it also finished my school days. For when I reached the age of 14 the lady who had visited us in Matilda St had taken me to her home for a few hours each day during the time my hand was healing. She had got my older brother into the Gas works as a patcher boy sometime previous to this. She was acquainted with the Gas manager Mr Stelfox. She had apprenticed me as a joiner to a firm of builders for 5 years. I was put to sandpapering the wooden parts that came off the machine for venetian blinds. I was receiving 2/6 weekly for this. I had been saving the few shillings I had received from friends during the time my hand was in a sling, and I decided that I would leave my trade and pay my fare to my uncle in Tyrone. When I arrived I had no idea where he lived in Omagh but I heard my father saying that everyone knew him, so when I mentioned his name to the first person I met, I was directed to a row of cottages outside the town. He was out and I had to wait; I am afraid I told a lie when I told him I had been unwell and I had been sent to him until I got better.

The three weeks I spent with him was very pleasant, every night neighbours arrive[d] and one brought a fiddle and we all sat round the open hearth with the turf fire; I was put in the hearth and enjoyed the yarns and the music. But I knew my days were numbered when I saw the postman and my uncle having a talk. He had received a letter from my mother and as my uncle like my father could not read or write, the postman had read the letter and he had been told to send me back to Belfast. I dreaded meeting my father who was waiting for me, but he made no reference to my running off. My uncle had given me a number of parcels to take home. I was welcomed like the lost prodigal. The lady who visited us often asked me on her next visit what I would like to work at. I told her that the Gas Department maintenance and distribution section had started a boy friend of mine, but you must be recommended. The following week I received a post card from the superintendent of the Gas Department, Queen Street, asking me to attend this office at 9.30, and bring my school certificates. This was the beginning of my career in the gas industry.

The superintendent examined my credentials and asked me a number of questions. This was my first encounter with a man who was to deal me some hard blows and who was to cause me a lot of grief and worry in later life. It was this man, as you will read later, that made me bitter against tyranny. I was told to report to the foreman. The Gas Department in Queen Street was where gas accounts were paid, and at the back of the building were the workshops into College Court. The foreman, Mr W. Gordon, took me upstairs and told another boy to show me how to paint gas meters. I was informed that this foreman was a socialist and not very popular. I was unaware at that time what a socialist meant. He is long dead and I must say that he treated me with kindness and consideration during the time he was alive. He was a sheet metal worker and taught a class in the technical school after he finished his work in the Gas Department.

At the time I commenced work in the Gas department, the employees were mostly sheet metal workers, a brass finisher, one plumber and I was one of about 4 boys. Two of us boys would fill a handcart with street lamps which the sheet metal workers had repaired and deliver them to the lamp stations. The lamplighters fitted them up. The lamplighters at that time lit the lamps with a hand lantern. I was sent out the second week with a meter fitter. The type of meter then was the wet type. Gas consumers at this time were the middle class and the upper class.

When I had been one year with a meter fitter and I had not received the shilling increase which boys were entitled to each year until they reached twenty-one, I told the foreman who promised to see the superintendent. Nothing extra was given to me the following week. So the foreman took me to see the superintendent. I was told that I would get my increase in due course. It was three months after when I received it without any back pay. During my first three years I only received two shillings instead of three. I had a talk with the other boys about this but as they were more interested in getting promoted to the complaint staff which would lead to Gas Inspector and the salary list I could make no impression so I decided to make application to Mr Nance for the position of tram conductor. I received in reply a letter from Mr Nance telling me to report to the depot in Sandy Row. Mr Nance had decided to start what he called a 'red duty'. He was putting on a number of cars to run on different roads from after 5 a.m. till 9.30 and from 12.30 till 2.30 and from 5 till 7 p.m. We had a red band around our uniform caps. The longest hours was Saturday where you took your car out at 1 o'clock. You did not arrive back at the depot until 8 but you had every Sunday off. I remained on this duty for two years when I was transferred to a regular duty in the Falls depot. I had married and I had to remove to Rockville [Street] to be close to the depot.

It was when I was put on this regular duty that I was reminded of my father's long hours. When I studied the hours I would work each week (over 72) it was only work and sleep. I asked some of the men in the depot if we could not get these hours reduced by starting a union but no one would listen to me. I was told if the manager heard about me trying to form a union I would be dismissed. Mason, my next door neighbour, an old driver who knew my father, warned me about the risk in talking about an organisation but I had made up my mind to join one, and I interviewed the late Alex Boyd who was organising municipal employees. I got my first card which I still have: it is dated the 11 Nov. 1907. I encouraged a few others to join, but later on they took cold feet and when I spoke to them they said their job was more important. I never lost an opportunity of trying to convince them that they were standing in their own light.

My bitterest opponent was my driver. To him I was an outlaw and a rebel. Previous to me taking over this duty there had been other conductors on this duty who had left and some had asked for a transfer as he was hard to work with. It was a transfer conductor duty when I took it over. I had been warned to watch out as he had made the others a life of hell. I was to find out the truth of that statement. Mr Nance had laid it down that the conductor was captain of the tram and the driver was under his control. The conductor was responsible for keeping his car up to schedule and was to send on a written report on accidents and all matters while on duty. You were issued with a report sheet, which you headed when making out a report: 'I beg leave to report' and you gave full particulars and the names of witnesses, and you finished up with 'I am your obedient servant'. My driver when I took over the car was very helpful, but I had noticed after a few weeks that he resented getting a bell after he had started the car. We had a number of discussions about this. He was in favour of the conductor turning his back on a passenger who ran after a car after it had started. I pointed out that we were public servants and the trams were for the use of the people and I also told him I was the one who would be reported not him. He would then refuse to speak to me and he made it very uncomfortable for if I was upstairs collecting fares and a passenger got on or off at a stop he would let the car stop until I came downstairs and rang the bell. He could tell when I was on the platform by looking into a shop window for when this mood came on him he usually stopped the car if a shop window was convenient.

He was trapped on one occasion coming down the Falls Road on the journey to Greencastle. I had a large number of passengers who were going to see the launch of the Titanic I believe. An inspector had boarded my car at the corner of the Springfield and Falls. The driver was unaware of this and when I was collecting fares on top he had refused to start when a post office messenger boy rang the bell so I had to come down and ring the bell myself. I did not notice the inspector sitting inside and it was only when I was collecting fares inside that he followed me out to the platform and asked me how long the driver had been carrying on this game. I told the inspector to ask the driver that question. When we came to the junction the inspector gave him a lecture; after that he would get friendly for some time and then start all over again.

He did not always get away with it. On one of my runs from Greencastle we timed our arrival to take on the passengers from a train at the Northern Counties railway. This train came in about 6.50 p.m. and when the driver was in a good mood he would arrive at the station in good time, and after the car was filled he would drive slowly along to the Castle Junction to give me an opportunity to collect the fares. But if he was not on speaking terms he would put on full speed with the result that it was impossible to have your fares, and passengers getting off at the Junction would hand you their fares. His object was to let the inspectors see these passengers giving me their fares and that I was neglecting my duty, but I decided that I would give him a run for his money. I had noticed a section box at one of the streets on our journey from the station and when a trolley is crossing a section box the driver must throw his controller handle to 'off' as a section of the overhead wire is dead. When I saw the driver throw the handle to 'off' I would throw the switch above my head to 'off' and that stopped the power until it was put on again. After I had done this I went on collecting fares and the driver had to leave the front of the car and put on the switch at my end. After I had done this for a few times he had to admit defeat.

On another occasion a lady came out of a street and signalled with her umbrella for him to stop. I was collecting fares on the top at the time. He told the lady she would be in good time for the next car. This lady happened to be the wife of a councillor and the driver did not know that. When my car returned to the junction I was called off by Inspector Rodgers, better known as 'Fiddler'. He told me that a lady had made a complaint against me with regard to a statement I had made to her. I denied all knowledge of it and claimed that I was being blamed in the wrong. I was told to carry on until I was put before the manager. When we arrived at our terminus our driver was anxious to know what was wrong. When I told him he made no comment, only 'Don't bother about it'. The next morning Inspector Rodgers was standing at Northern Counties station waiting for my car coming from Greencastle. I expected that this was my summons to go before the manager. After I had collected the fares he asked me if I had told my driver about my case. I told him I had, and he asked me what the driver had said in reply. When I told him he said, 'I have to apologise to you for blaming you in the wrong'. The lady afterwards when she arrived home told her husband she had blamed the conductor instead of the driver and the husband had come down to the Junction at night and reported what his wife had told him. I was off duty and did not know until the following morning. My driver was suspended for a week for this, not so much for what he had said but for keeping quiet when he knew I was blamed in the wrong. That afternoon Councillor J. Doran[8] boarded my car and apologised to me on behalf of his wife and he told me to call on him if ever I required any help in Corporation matters.

Mr Nance was a man that believed the passenger was right until you could prove otherwise. He was ruthless and very drastic in punishing his employees. During my 5½ years' service I never had occasion to be brought before him but I have known numerous cases of trammies receiving hard sentences for trivial offences. My driver in red duty days lost a ½d [half-penny] an hour for three months because he knocked a splinter off the lifeguard when he was trying his car in the depot before starting off and my next door neighbour was an old tram driver who had given good service even under the old Company yet, when he stopped a runaway pony which a young lady was driving and had lost control, he was suspended by Mr Nance for a week because he did not report the matter which his conductor did. This man could not read or write and like my father he would have went anywhere and at all times if the manager had asked him. When I stormed with regard to this injustice he would not listen to anything I said against Mr Nance. This was the class of men I tried to organise.

You were given a special duty board on Easter Monday and Tuesday and the 12th July and 13th. Printed on the top of this special duty were the words in red ink: 'No relief', that meant from 7 a.m. till 11.30 p.m. without food. Still no one would protest against this treatment. During my time we had no covered trams. There was half a roof to cover you and the drivers were issued with sou'westers. The drivers had to face all weather and the conductors when not collecting fares stood beneath the stairs to keep the rain off. When you had completed twelve hours under these conditions you were ready for a rest. There were points in Nance's favour. You were rewarded each Xmas with two sovereigns if your receipts were correct for the twelve months: I received this on a number of Xmases. And another one was a sovereign to the drivers who were free from any accident during the year and he also rewarded any driver who saved a life or averted an accident. The following will serve to show.

My driver had been suspended and a spare man[9] took over the car. This man told me that he had been out of work for a long time before he got engaged on the trams. There was no dole in those days and this man had a wife and children but it was your friends and neighbours who helped you until you were lucky to get work. I had noticed that his boots were far beyond repair but he was very cheerful and glad to get work. His only dread was the fear of an accident and he was using the emergency brake at the slightest sign of danger. Coming down the Falls

Road opposite the Model School a little girl ran across in front of the car and the driver applied the emergency brake which upset the passengers inside the car. One of the passengers was a well known wine merchant. I told him the reason for the emergency brake and when he was getting off at the Junction I asked him if he would report the matter to one of the Inspectors. On my return journey an Inspector boarded my car and questioned me with regard to the matter: he said it had been reported at the Junction and I would have to make out a report for the manager. This was what I was wishing for. Two days after I had sent in my report the driver received a sovereign. He wanted to divide it with me but I told him to buy a pair of boots. And another spare driver I had who was taking the place of drivers on holidays. This man was a well known boxer. We were issued with white tops in the summer time. We were rounding the Junction from the Falls Road into Royal Avenue and the driver had gonged at a man who was crossing in front of his car. The driver told me afterwards that the man said to him, 'Take your time Ice Cream'. The driver left his car and toed this man at the corner of Bank Street. He was taken off the car and that was the finish of his career on the trams.

[*Here McElborough recounts two further anecdotes relating to tramway staff. Circa 500 words.*]

I will give my experience with regard to the public from a conductor's point. My four duties were Andersonstown, Greencastle, Balmoral and Cregagh. The people on the Falls were as a rule helpful in giving you their fare before going on top. I was known personally to the Rev. Gibson, Broadway, Fr Convery, St Paul's, the McDonnells father and son, Heatherington, Broadway, director, McGinley, mineral water manufacturer, a number of others who were well known about the Falls Road. They all treated me with kindness and goodwill. The Greencastle people were working class with the exception of Mr T. Gallaher of tobacco fame who was often a passenger and I had one dispute with him.[10] He had been walking between the stops and when the driver rightly ignored his signal to stop it was I who received the dressing down from him when he boarded the car. He threatened to report me and I pointed out that the driver was right not to stop but I afterwards told the driver if he met him again in the same position he had better stop as his report to the manager would carry weight. But he was always at a stop after that. If he was coming up from Whitehouse in the morning, I had to wait until he got on the car even if I was late in starting. But the Greencastle route recalls to memory a passenger who had been in the habit of giving a pound note to conductors for a twopenny ticket on the first run in the morning. Conductors when we finished at night had been talking about this client. As they were unable to change the pound note he got his ticket for nothing as the conductors stated he never took the same car twice. I kept when working this early duty 19/– in coppers in a bag in case I would meet him, and it was a long time before I met him. I recognised him the morning he boarded my car as he bid me good morning, but when he apologised for having only a pound note, I told him it was alright and I would change it. He was surprised and when I counted 19/– on the window ledge he received a shock. He asked me if I could not give him silver and when I told him that this was my first run he knew the £1 game was up. I received a vote of thanks when I told the other conductors in the depot.

There was one passenger on the Balmoral run that got on my car some mornings at 9 a.m. It was remarkable to see him running out of one of the avenues with his collar and tie in his hand which he put on when he got upstairs, He never had his fare and he excused himself by saying that he left his money in his other clothes. This happened a number of times but when he did pay his fare occasionally he made no attempt to pay up for the ones he had previously got and I did not like to remind him in front of the other passengers. It was worth twopence to see him running after the car with his collar and tie in his hand. He confessed to me one morning when getting off the car at the Cooke statue[11] that if he missed this car he would lose a day. I often wondered if he ever got his breakfast.

The only other complaint I had against the Balmoral run was the journey from Balmoral to Northern Counties Railway in the holiday period. On an afternoon journey the people at every stop on your journey had large luggage cases for the Northern Counties Railway. It was impossible to take them on the platform. I must have had my badge number taken by thousands of passengers during the years I was on that run. Some of them to make me shiver promised to see their friend my manager. I had suggested a luggage trailer behind my car and to charge passengers twopence for each bag. My suggestion I suppose went no further than the Inspector I mentioned it to.

The Inspector staff in my time was small but they certainly had their work cut out. It was the parade to the Balmoral Showgrounds of the Unionist clubs from all over Ireland that decided me to leave the trams [1912].[12] I left the depot on that morning and I did not return home until almost 1 a.m. the following morning. My wife had went out on a number of occasions during the day with food for me but failed to find me and when I arrived home I wrote out my resignation and sent it to the Junction.[13] The manager sent for me and wanted to know the reason for my resignation. I told him I was going to another job. He told me he insisted on employees working a two-week notice but owing to my good record he would overlook this and if I would return my uniform tomorrow I would receive a fortnight's wages and if I wanted a reference to my new employers he would give it to me. He said he did not make a rule of giving references. His reference which I have before me as I write states:

> 'R. McElborough has asked me for a reference. His father was a faithful and valued servant of the Belfast Tramway Company. His son Robert entered the service in—[1907] as a tram conductor. He has left on his own request after five and a half years' service. During this period I found him honest, trustworthy and he carried out his duties faithfully. I can confidently recommend him.'

Before leaving his office he told me that if I did not like my new job he was prepared to reinstate me with my service, which meant I would receive the full rate of pay. At that time a conductor had to complete three years before receiving the full rate and the gold band.

I had made up my mind before I resigned that I would interview Councillor J. Doran who was Chairman of the Gas Committee and ask him to get me back to the Gas Department. When I interviewed him I told him I had left the trams and that I had completed over three years as a boy in the Gas Department. I told him the reasons why I had left— the long hours and restrictions under which men had to work and you never had a day off duty. He told me to call and see him in a few days, and he gave me a lecture on giving up one job before taking up another. When I called on him again, I was handed a letter to take to the superintendent of the Maintenance Department and I was started as a competent meter changer or fitter.

Just before I had decided to leave the trams Jim Larkin had come over from Liverpool to organise the dockers and not getting any encouragement from the shipping owners with regard to wages and conditions Larkin decided to strike by bringing out the dockers, and the owners brought in the police and the military [1907]. Our organizer took the dockers' side and he was condemned. He got up collections amongst the members of the Municipal Employees and we gave what assistance we could to the dockers in their fight. I had been getting very frequent visits from the Inspectors during the dockers' strike and the conversation was on Larkin and how he was upsetting lorries of food and defying law and order, but I had the opinion that these Inspectors were fishing to hear my views for the purpose of reporting to higher ups. But I was careful and when some Inspectors condemned my organizer for interfering I made no comment. There was no dole in those days and men had to consider their homes and their children. However the dockers won after a hard and severe struggle. It was the forming of the dockers union under Ben Tillett whom I was to meet later in life. This victory also put a bit of courage into the small band of Municipal workers for when we met afterwards in a small room in Fountain Lane above Hannigans public house we received a letter of thanks from the dockers union for our help and assistance. But our organizer who was a representative on the City Council lost his seat for St George's ward. All the help he had given to the dockers and the destruction of food by the strikers and the loss of thousands of pounds by the city was cast against him during this election and it was a sad blow to the members of the M E A when he was defeated. A large number left the union. When he was a member of the council he was successful in getting the Municipal Employees Association, for the collecting steward D. Gordon had to stand on the street outside the Gas Works for years. Dennis Houston, an organizer from Glasgow, had tried to get the gas manager to allow a man to collect the contributions but failed. We were looked upon as a lot of hooligans who were trying to rob the workman of some of his hard earned wages. My position in the maintenance was worse as I had no one in that department in the Union. For me to approach any of the workers on the question was committing suicide and having no representative on the council to take up your case if you were dismissed. And I was advised when I raised this matter at our meetings to wait until things settled down. But strange to relate my opportunity came sooner than I expected.

The department had began to light parts of the city with fittings and hanging mantles which the Welsbach Company had introduced. The four men who were appointed to this work had been getting a number of wet days and they approached the superintendent to ask him if they could not be supplied with waterproofs. He turned their request down. I suggested that they interview my organizer of the Chairman of the Gas Committee, Councillor J. Doran. A few days later they decided to see Doran who promised to bring the matter before the Gas Committee. The following week the foreman told them the superintendent wished to see them, and after a stormy interview they were handed chits and told to go and be fitted with a waterproof. It was a victory and the first one and I tried to point out that unity had won, but they would not agree to join the union as they said I was not present at the interview, so I was not a marked man like them. I told them that it was my intention to ask for a waterproof also as I was out all day with a handcart full of meters. When I approached the foreman with regard to a waterproof he warned me against it and told me that the office knew that I had advised the four men to see the chairman and that it was known that I held a union card and if I were paid off I would be on the streets.

In the meantime the foreman's health was bad and there were a lot of secret meetings being held and a vigilate [*vigilance*] committee had been formed for the purpose of appointing a foreman to replace Gordon with a loyalist. The new chairman of the Gas Committee was a councillor named Craig and I used to see him and a few others who were employed in the Gas department talking together outside the City Hall in the evening.[14] One of this group was afterwards appointed foreman in my department and another man was made foreman in the stove warehouse and the third one was made coke seller in the gas works: this man had a grocer shop.

It was the system in the gas department during my young days that promotion to the complaint staff was seniority and ability. You had to have a knowledge of gas meters and complaints with regard to bad pressure and to trace escapes and to level off the meter if the water failed to act on the drum. Promotion was slow as the consumers in the city were middle and high class, and the meter inspectors staff were about 6 and a few complaint men. The inspector staff were on the salaries list which meant a pension on retiring. The complaint staff moved into any vacancy that secured in the inspectors' staff and the worker was promoted to the complaint staff.

Long before I left the department for the trams, the auto or slot meter had been introduced and applications were coming in from the working class in thousands. It meant laying service mains all over the city and the department, which up to then had been a nice easy going concern, became a hive of activity. There were a large number of boys and men started and I was sent out with a sheet metal worker to fit up slot meters.

This man was a gas fitter who had, along with others, got engaged to do this work as I had been out with some of the permanent workers who fitted up gas cookers and other gas appliances previous to the introduction of the autometer. I was expected to show my knowledge to this new man. He told me he had been working in one of the down-town shops and he had only a light knowledge of gas fitting and none of meter fitting. He gave me a good tip every weekend during the time I worked with him. I want to say that I earned it. I was caught a number of times by an official who was following these men. I knew he gave him a lecture, but this man, without my help, would have been useless.

These sheet metal workers and the plumbers had a battle royal about their rights to do this work and the superintendent enjoyed it as it resulted in the two class of workers engaged against each other. The plumbers, when they were returning from their day's work to the office, kept to themselves the number of meters they had fitted up and when the week-end arrived the superintendent would have sent for some of the sheet metal workers and told them that unless they returned more work they would have to go. As the plumbers were not sent for, the blame was on the plumbers. The result of this opposition in the two camps was that we were made to load hand carts with meters, grillers, stands and pipings and to take this load out each morning. Previous to these hand carts, these meters and fittings were delivered at the house by a horse and van, but the fight for who would do most made the van delivery too slow to keep up with the rush.

A number of boys had been started but when the handcarts were introduced it was the cause of some of them leaving as the small wage we were receiving resulted in a lot of trouble. Some of these boys, to be free of the handcarts, slept in till breakfast time, but the foreman sent a man with the handcart to the first job and when the boy came in at breakfast time, he was packed off to relieve this man.

Some of these boys were friends of members of the council and some were friends of friends of the council. The foreman, to his credit, made no distinction, but I was under the opinion he was often discussed and condemned for making some of these special boys push a handcart. It is easily understood, the haste that was made to appoint a man who had taken a prominent part in the vigilant committee when the foreman took ill. And when he disappointed them later by returning to work, they ask[ed] him to be assistant foreman, owing to his health. He refused and the foreman who had been holding his position was appointed to be outside foreman. The foreman took ill twice afterwards and died. The position of affairs up till his death reminded me of the vultures I had read about who kept watch until their victim collapsed.

The[re] was a boy started during this foreman['s] time who was the son of a poor law guardian. He refused to push a handcart and the foreman sent for him. This caused fireworks. The boy had told me that his father had got him into the Gas department to become a Gas Inspector. The following morning after his dismissal, he came back. He remained inside until the first appointments were made for auto meter Inspectors. He and a few others who had started a long time after me were appointed. These appointments caused a lot of discussion in the old Town Hall in Victoria Street w[h]ere the council met. Councillors Walker and E. MacGuinness, the two Labour members, wanted a full inquiry into these appointments. It was decided to have an examination and I decided that I would forward my name for this examination. I consulted the foreman who told me to hand in my name to the Superintendent. This action caused another scene, as the Superintendent told me that I would not get his permission as I had to attend to my work and I would have to lose a day's pay if I attended the examination. The following day the foreman told me that I would get away. He had been interviewing the Superintendent and had pointed out that a number of other boys had been attending and he would have to allow me also, but he told me confidentially that I stood no chance because these appointments were already made and the Superintendent was annoyed because I had dared to make application for an official position. The salary for this position was £104 per annum. At that time craftsmen's wages were 36 shillings weekly, labourers 18/6, boys 10/6.

The examination was held in the Technical School and it snowed all day and my boots were not watertight. I had to sit at a desk and do a number of sums. The additions and subtractions were alright and the reading of the index of the three meters, but the catch was the fraction sums. What they had to do with collecting pennies out of slot meters was beyond me, but I knew I was not in the hunt, so I handed in my paper. The result was as the foreman said. I received a reply from an official telling me that I had been unsuccessful. But I was to get my own back with these people years later in an examination when I was older and wiser. This examination was the beginning of who you know and not what you know. The Poor Law Guardian's son who was amongst the successful gas inspectors did not reign [long] in that position. Just before I transferred to the trams, he had made away with some of the gas collections. He went to America and no more was heard of him.

When I restarted [1913] after my 5½ years on the trams I found a lot of changes had taken place. The plumbers had won their battle with the sheet metal workers who were working inside at the bench, but there were two brassfinishers who were outside repairing gas escapes and the plumbers were still kept at a big number of jobs each day. Some of these jobs were a scandal. The piping that led from the meter to the gas bracket was tied to cord with nails in the wall. In one of the houses that I had to change a meter, the plumber had fitted a gas cooker underneath the meter which was on a shelf. When I told the plumber who had done this about the danger if the cooker was lit beneath the meter he asked me not to speak about it and he would call round after working hours with piping and alter the position of the cooker. It was providence that prevented a number of gas accidents.

The main layers were not to blame for the positions they laid the service [pipes] in a large number of dwelling houses and shops. Their instructions were to fit the service pipe inside the outside wall of a dwelling or shop. Some were fitted in cupboards and underneath shop counters. Those who were engaged in fitting and changing these meters and fittings were often gassed. In a confined space like a cupboard we had to work over an open service pipe and under a shop counter we were in the same position. It was impossible to take a light with us and we had to grope in the dark to feel for the fittings that we had to change. In the case of the changing of meters in these positions, we had to turn the service cock to blow the air out of a new meter before the meter filled up with gas.

I have lost count of the number of times I came out of these positions like a drunken man, and many times I lay unconscious for fifteen minutes before I came round. But when you are young you forget about it. Some of the men who were older had to go to hospital when they were gassed but they were not detained after treatment. I used to imagine when I saw old meter fitters staggering like drunk men as they talked, that they were drunk, but after forty-one years of experience I know what was the matter. I have experienced the attacks of dizziness and vomiting as I got on in years and lost all my energy. I had this feeling for a long time before I had to give up.

When I again entered the Gas Department, I was told to take up meter fitting and changing. I had a boy with me and when the street lighting was extended I was sent to fit up lamps. In the meantime I had attended the meetings of the union. All municipal employees were together. We were only a few hundred strong and our organiser Alex Boyd had a hard task. He was hearing every meeting tales of victimisation and he gave us a lot of advice. Some of our meetings in the Engineers' Hall in College Street was like a bear garden on a Saturday evening under the chairmanship of Alex Bowman.[15] When I look back over these years and contrast them with the present time, I often wonder if the present members of trade unions and their officials realise the hard road and the opposition from our fellow workers, the bosses and the press, and the victimisation we pioneers had to stand. Our officials were receiving 25/– weekly and they were out in all weathers. I have known Alex Boyd to go to a pumping station near midnight to hear a complaint from [members]. There was no distance too far or no complaint that he did not investigate. When we were short of funds through paying victimisation benefit, we used to run a ballot among ourselves to raise a few pounds. When Alex stood for the City Council on the second occasion he topped the poll over the rest of the candidates. He was made Alderman: this election was under Proportional Representation. It was a sad blow to the workers in the Gas Department when he died undergoing an operation. He knew his subject, gas, as a stoker, and during the time he was a member of the gas Committee he got things done for the worker: the manager had to pay attention to any complaints he brought forward.

[*Here McElborough recounts the difficulties of a collecting steward and describes an incident in which a union official struck a manager and was dismissed.* Circa 480 words.]

We were receiving reports from Will Thorne about victories he had won at the Brecton [Beckton] London gas undertaking. This was the gas works he had been employed in as a stoker when he formed the Gas-workers Union. His other victory was in the Leeds gasworks. He had been arrested when leading the strikers and had refused to be bound over to keep the peace. We had decided at this meeting to invite Will Thorne to address a meeting that we intended to hold on the first day of May [1893] in the Ormeau Park. Some were in favour of taking part in a parade and after discussion this matter was left optional. It required courage to take part in a march.

Will Thorne arrived from London via Fleetwood, 3rd [class rail] and steerage [on the boat]. It was his first visit to Ireland and we were intro-duced all round. He gave us a lot of courage after he had told us about the progress he was making in building up the Municipal Employees Association. He had brought along a green sash with the Municipal Employees Association badge on it. It was this sash that nearly caused a riot in Ormeau Park. Will, not being aware of political feeling in Ire-land, could not understand why the wearing of a green sash would annoy the workers. He was on one of the park seats after he had addressed the meeting with his sash still on when a number of men asked him if he was a member of the Fenian society. Will, thinking that this was some trade union, told them he was a member of the Munic-ipal Employees Association and pointed to his badge. By this time a crowd had collected and it took some persuasion before we could res-cue Will. To explain to him about Home Rule and his sash was beyond us. Many times afterwards when I visited his office in Ponders End and later in Tavistock Square, his secretary (for Will could not read or write) used to enjoy hearing about the part where Will was taken for a member of the Home Rule movement.

His visit to Belfast did good amongst the men of the manufacturing section, but my section was still miles behind, I would enrol six this week and the following week [they] would drop out. Someone would speak to them about me being warned by the bosses.

It was heartbreaking to think that we were unable to seek an increase or to better our conditions. If we got Easter Monday as a holiday we had to start work on Easter Tuesday at 6, otherwise we lost Monday's pay, even if we came in at breakfast time. This rule applied to the 12th July and Christmas one day holiday also. The Corporation had passed this as a concession. In my young days the rule for these three holidays were: the departments closed down at one o'clock and we were free for the afternoon. As for the officials, they received a week's holiday with pay. After 10 years' service they received 12 days, after 20 years they were entitled to three weeks, and so on for every 10 years' service, while the heads of the departments received a month's holiday. but it required a strike in the Gas Works before we made any progress.

We had been removing our union rooms all over the city. We sometimes received notice to quit. Between these removals we had to elect an organiser. The gasworkers had asked me to stand but I declined on the grounds of being incompetent. What a joke on me this statement is after 40 years membership and hearing union officials. There was no question that I would have been elected. The gasworks vote at that time was a winner and I was well known to the gasworkers at our meetings. When I refused to be nominated, F. Lutton, a lamplighter, decided to go forward. He at that time was unknown to the gasworkers as he did not attend any meetings. He was one of the pioneers of our union and of a quiet type. The other nomination for this position was J. Malcolm who was employed in the Corporation park. He was unknown to me or any of the gasworkers of that period but he was all out to be elected. Lutton did no canvassing but not so Malcolm, who beat Lutton by a majority of a little over 30, I had expected a larger majority considering the amount of time and the energy expended.

Lutton was to be in control of the ledger and finance and to look after all correspondence. He would come up every three years for election. In his vote of thanks to the members for electing him he promised to carry out his duties faithfully and, as he stated, 'I am your servant to command'.

His first big test came when the gasworkers came out on strike [1918]. His job was difficult because some of the lamplighting staff volunteered to work in the gasworks, and I was sorry for him when we met each morning on the rooms in Arthur Place. Lamplighters who were loyal to the Union attended these morning meetings and urged drastic action against these men. We had arranged to supply the hospitals with gas during the strike and had selected a number of men to carry out these duties but the manager refused our offer as he believed he could smash the strike. The Gas Committee gave the manager a free hand and unlimited funds. He supplied the strike breakers with new boiler suits and he engaged a catering firm to set up a canteen to feed the strike breakers.

Very few of these men went home. Those that remained all night in the works were provided with beds but any who did venture out got it hot and heavy. One man who belonged to my department who left for home by the back gate was caught and the fact that he had a club foot saved him from being thrown into the river Lagan. He pleaded his large family and he promised not to return to the gasworks, but the following morning he had an escort of police to protect him from his home to the works and back at night. This man was rewarded later with a Gas official's position. Another man whom the strikers discovered before the police knew received a severe mauling and they stripped him and raffled his new boiler suit.

We were receiving information that the strike breakers were no use in the retort house[16]. My superintendent had asked for volunteers for strike breaking. He had decided to call the roll and as our name was called we went past the time office. We were to signify 'yes' or 'no'. When this notice was put up I did everything possible to influence the workers not to blackleg. They were told the department would close down and workers would be started again as required. When I tried to convince these men to remain out they told me that not being members of the Union they would not receive strike pay. I promised them if they would refuse to work in the gasworks I would guarantee to get them strike pay. I had no authority for making this statement and it cost me a few sleepless nights for the men refused to blackleg. We had been receiving money from our fellow-workers in England and when I received word from London through our organiser to pay the non-union men strike pay I was delighted.

This strike was finished after two weeks, but our victory was bought very dear. When we turned up to work the morning after our instructions to start work, the superintendent cleared us all out and shut the gate. It was I and another member named T. Boyd who became our chairman later on, that stood the brunt of this mean attack that morning. He had threatened us with the police for daring to tell the workmen to start without his authority. I told Boyd not to reply as he only wanted an opportunity to dismiss him. During the strike the superintendent had taken two boys, one in each hand, over to the gasworks, and Boyd and I tried to take the boys away from him telling the boys that they were going to blackleg. He called the police who ordered us away.

When the superintendent put us out he crossed over to the gasworks to have a confab with the superintendent of the gasworks. As the manager did not arrive until 9.30 some of the men decided to wait but I went home, and when I turned up at breakfast time, the superintendent had instructed the foreman to make us line up and answer the roll call. When the names of the men who were engaged on lamp fittings and repairs were called they were told to stand to one side. I was engaged in fitting and changing meters and I was passed on with an angry look and T. Boyd, who was employed in the meter testing shop was passed on with the same look. I was anxious to hear of the fate of these lamp maintenance men. After he had completed the roll call, he told these men there would be no work for them for some considerable time and he would send for them if he required them. He had not forgotten these men going to the chairman for waterproofs.

We had won a great victory and the price had been dear. I had the case of these men taken before the manager but failed to get them started. Two of these men got back six months later and the rest went to other work. One of the two who got started through a councillor was sent to the pipe-laying squad on the street and the other man was sent to do watchman at oil boats and was gradually put on the high pressure lamps that had been fitted around the City Hall.

The first meeting of our union after the strike lasted to midnight, hearing complaints about the mess the plant had been left, and also cases of victimisation, but the one outstanding thing was—we had been recognised after years of hard fighting. An agreement was to be drawn up between the manager and our union and to be submitted to us for approval, and I was able to report a substantial increase in membership in my department. The non-union men who had received strike pay had signed up.

The winning of the strike had been like a tonic to municipal workers as the organizer had reported great progress. We had to remove from Arthur Place to East Bridge Street and it was here that we received word from our London office to form branches for each department and to elect a chairman, secretary, auditors and a branch committee. As our organizer had too large a membership he was restricted in his work of organising. The instructions were to number the branches according to their membership. As the gas department had the largest number of members we were No. 1 in the Irish district. I had been doing minute secretary under the old system at 10/− per quarter. I was asked by the new branch Secretary to carry on. I declined a number of branch positions that night. But I had received a vote of thanks for the good work in organising so many in my department. I was to receive congratulations later on from T. Boyd on a hundred per cent membership and asked [?] him to take over the collecting steward book as he was an indoor man, and had better facilities for meeting the members than I had.

[*Here McElborough pays tribute to T. Boyd with whom he had worked in developing trade unionism in the gas industry. Circa 410 words.*]

But I am rather advanced in my story, as I wish to go back to my tramway days [ca. 1907] to tell about the time I joined the Ulster Liberal

Association whose headquarters were in the Central Hall, Rosemary Street.[17] It issued a weekly paper called the 'Ulster Guardian'.[18] To be anything but a Unionist or a Nationalist in those days required courage but I was attracted when I read this paper about the debates on the principal things that concerned the betterment of the workers' lives. Campbell Bannerman had been returned to power later, after I had joined, but previous to this we had some great debates on houses and National Insurance which was to become law years later.[19] Mr McDowell was the organizing Secretary of this association. He was a splendid speaker and I tried to interest him in a workers' movement, but nothing would induce him to leave the Liberal party. His argument was that the workers should join the Liberal party and he pointed to John Burns[20] and a miner named Burt[21] who had been returned to the Commons as Liberal-Labour and Joseph Arch.[22] But I had taken part in a discussion on Arch whose life I had read. He organized the farm labourers of Norfolk and he spent his life pleading the workers' cause. It was he who got the worker the franchise. He founded the National Agricultural Labourers union and succeeded in obtaining a general rise in wages and reform on various abuses. He was returned to parliament as member for West Norfolk. I told Mr McDowell if he would only come out into the open and urge the worker to organize, he would succeed. I invited him to attend one of our meetings in the engineers hall and hear our complaints. He might change his mind. He was very interested in the workers being organised but he thought the organisers should come from the workers, that men who were engaged in the work would be the proper persons to meet the managers or directors of business concerns. The discussion on this matter was interesting, owing to the fact that there were a large number of businessmen in the room who agreed that they would rather have a round table talk with their workmen than outside officials providing their demands were reasonable.

I enjoyed these discussions for we had speakers like T. W. Russell, MP, Young MP[23], Glendinning MP[24] and W. Redmond MP[25], and a number of others. We had a visit from Lord Dunraven[26] who had a plan for satisfying both sides on the Home Rule question. What I liked about the Ulster Liberal Party was the free for all discussion that followed the address. If you were in favour of retaining the British connection you were afforded every facility to state your view. The nationalist members who visited us were of a different type than the present. The church did not control them to the same extent as today. I can imagine what would happen if three Orange lodges on the 12th of July morning passed by St Paul's on the Falls Road and down the Grosvenor Road headed by a band and Father Convery PP standing at his manse looking on.[27] Yet for years this route was insisted on by Father Convery. I had lived in Rockville Street on the Falls Road and the street was mixed but religion was never mentioned at any time. My Roman Catholic friends are legion, but it was the invitation to Winston Churchill who was in the Liberal cabinet that smashed the Ulster Liberal party [1912].

I made my protest against him coming to Belfast and resigned. I had been secretary of the South Belfast branch which had been gaining strength every month. It is my conviction that Ireland would have remained under the union and that a plan would have been formed that would have satisfied North and South. The Irish MPs North and South at that time could have made as good an agreement as we have at present without any blood being shed, but bringing over an Englishman who had no knowledge of Ireland, it was a big blunder and it was the finish of my taking part in political parties. When I look back on them, I believe the Liberal party was wrecked on the Irish question. I have been in England more times than I can remember and I have been in many discussions with English people on the Irish question, and the majority of them were like Will Thorne who thought when he had appeared in a green sash that all Irishmen would welcome him, but he like other Englishmen who visited Ireland a few times and talked with the people found out that there were two Irelands because when I visited Thorne in the Wembley exhibition year [1924], I asked him to show me round the House of Commons. He said he had arranged for a man and his wife from Dublin to show them also, and when we all met the following day, Thorne introduced us to to each other as orange and green and hoped we would not fight until after he had shown us round.

I reminded him on my next visit to London that the North contained thousands of green as well as orange, and he said I thought I was being educated on the Irish question.

I have had some exciting times in Hyde Park when I have had my collar and tie torn when the police decided to break up a meeting which I had considered to be quiet when Englishmen speak on the Irish question. I am only giving a brief outline of these things, but in my other manuscript I have given particulars.

Well that is about all I had to do with politics, so I will resume my trade union and my gas department experience . . .

[*Here McElborough describes his work training boys in meter fitting. This provides him with an opportunity to expound on his belief that many were friends or relatives of councillors and aldermen.* Circa 1800 words.]

We had been told to number our jobs and to leave a copy in the office before we took out our cart or meters. It happened that my first job was a provision shop in Cromac Street and I had to change a fifth fitting. The meter was like thousands of other meters in shops. It was below the window next the street and there was a large marble slab above it. I had to crawl underneath this slab on my stomach to disconnect the cock and the fitting. You had to work in the dark and after I had disconnected it I had to fit on the new one. I always carried a cork for when I felt the gas overcoming me, I put the cork in the service until the boy pulled me out until I recovered from the effects of the gas in my system. At the second attempt I succeeded in getting the thread of the cock on the service [pipe]. I remembered nothing more until I recovered and saw my own boy and the shop boy and the Inspector. I always told my boy when I kicked with my foot to pull me out. As this was the first visit of this Inspector to me he was certainly scared stiff, as he told me he thought I was dead as I was a long time coming round. He wanted me to go to hospital, but I told him that I had often been gassed underneath shops and in cupboards. He must have reported the matter for I did not see him again for a long time. I was telling the other meter fitters about the shock he got on his first visit. I brought this matter of gas poisoning to try and get it remedied. I even offered myself to be x-rayed, but it was only lost time as the organiser had no knowledge of meter fitting. And it was only when two of my work-mates were found dead that the department began to take notice. I would have liked to have got giving evidence at the inquest. These two fellow-workers were working over an open service pipe. The first workman had sent his boy to get him a piece of piping underneath where he was working and when the boy went to hand it to him, he found he was dead. The gas had overcome him. He left a wife and family. The other workman, a few years later, was found in the same position, only this case was a new house where he had to fit a meter. He had got the key from a neighbour who when her husband came in for dinner told him that the key of the new house had not been returned by the gasman. The husband forced the lock of the door and found him dead over an open service. He had no boy with him and his mother fainted at the inquest. This was a young man starting in life. I have had to give up this work, still I have not given up hope that something will be done to protect the workers in this important part of the Gas Industry.

During the first world war the boys had decided that their wages were no use and one morning they refused to take out the carts with the meters. The foreman tried to reason with them but they refused to listen. The superintendent then came on the scene and gave them 2 minutes to get the carts out. They would have won as boys were scarce but unfortunately some of these boys were favourites for promotion. It was these boys who were first out with the carts. I was of course looked upon as the one who had caused this trouble, which led to me being sent to look after a gas engine which drove the high pressure lamps around the City Hall. The man who was engaged on this had met with an injury and was taken to the hospital. When I asked the foreman why he had selected me, he said I would only be a few weeks there until the man retired. I took over this job on this condition.

It was during the time that I was on this job that De Valera, who up to then had been stirring up trouble in the south, had announced that he would hold a meeting in the waste ground in College Street opposite the building where I was in charge of the gas engine.

This meeting was advertised to commence at 10p.m. 13th [*recte*, 16th] March [1918], the following day being Sunday St Patrick's day. All political meetings had been banned. This was 1915 [*recte*, 1918].[28] I was warned by the authorities who expected trouble to remain indoors at my engine but as St Patrick's day did not commence until after 12 p.m. according to the notice issued from Dublin Castle by the British Government, I decided to hear what De Valera had to say about Ireland. The platform, which was a four-wheel lorry, was drawn up close to the yards walls in King Street. I noticed by the light of the torches that his supporters carried that the platform party could easily escape into King Street if they decided to carry on the meeting after 12 p.m. On the platform with de Valera was McEntee, whose father had a public house in King Street, which I was often in when our workshops were in College Street. One of our old plumbers, R. Rooney, used to bring his fiddle to this public house after working hours and entertain us in the back parlour. Old McEntee, the father, and W. Connor, a sheet metal worker in our department, whose son is drawing lifelike sketches of types of Ulster workers[29], and a few others enjoyed many happy nights.

After I had heard de Valera speak, I cleared back to my engine for the crowd was telling him to defy the Government ban. When 12 struck the head of the police went up to the platform to ask the party to close the meeting, but they decided to carry on. The police who were there in hundreds carried out their instructions but it was the unfortunate supporters who received the full force of this battle. I had stationed myself at one of the windows in the engine room. I could not see but I heard the cracks of batons and heard the ambulances taking away the wounded to hospital. It was 3 a.m. when the police told me that I could come out as it was all over. As it was dark, I picked up one of the torches and lit it to survey the battlefield. What a sight. Hats, caps, sticks, badges, scarves, pipes were all around the waste ground. I filled my arms with these and placed them in the engine room where they lay for many weeks after being viewed by the workers in the department. De Valera, McEntee and Dr McNabb of the platform party got away, but it was months before some of the crowd who attended that meeting left the hospital.

With regard to his speech, after I had heard a large number of speakers of the old Irish parliamentary party I would not class de Valera in the same category. I would say that his speech that night was something like what Arthur Trew, of Customs House steps fame, would make.[30] I can sympathise with supporters of the old nationalist party in that they believed in winning Ireland North and South without the sword. No more can a southern Irishman tell the Northman that a Dutchman had to lead them, for they won't have an outsider in charge of their government. My mother had told when she was a little girl her people and other relations left Tyrone for USA and how they took up arms on behalf of America against Britain because they believed that Britain was wrong in which history has since then agreed. I have had many discussions with southern Irishmen on the Irish question but I have seldom heard two agree on the method they would employ to win the North and that is one of the reasons that, since my liberal days, I remained a no-party man but have devoted my life to the betterment of my fellow-worker.

During the months I looked after the gas engine, I was kept informed by my work-mates about what was taking place in the workshops, how the privileged few were being promoted and that it was the intention of the bosses to keep me in this position. The next visit I had from the foreman I asked him when the other man who had started in the workshops was coming back to his job again. He told me that the fitting of meters was very slack and that I was alright where I was. I reminded him of his promise when he asked me to do this job and that the man was fit to take over. I waited for another week without getting any word. The foreman who used to call on me one night in the week stopped, so I decided to get a move on.

Lloyd George had been calling for volunteers for war work. We were not allowed to join the army, after the war had been well advanced. They had made the Gas Industry a key industry, so I made inquiries for the purpose of finding out if I volunteered for war work would I be entitled to get back my job and my service in the gas department. After receiving an assurance on this matter, I filled and forwarded a volunteer form to the Government. I received back a reply telling me to present myself at the main office, Harland & Wolff, and to bring this letter with me. Being off work through the day I had to ask no boss for permission. I was interviewed at Harland & Wolff and I was asked what I could do. I told them what I was employed in at the gas department and they asked me if I would take up a foundry crane to learn. I was told to give the gas department notice so I told the foreman the following morning in the workshop that I was leaving on Saturday. He would not take me seriously and told me to go home to bed. What a shock he got on Saturday when I demanded my cards. He told me after I had told him where I was going that I was finished with the gas department; I made no reply. I was told afterwards that he had to send his man back to the gas engine. After the war I presented myself to the foreman in the gas department to ask for my job back. He told me there was no job for me. I told him to see the superintendent and on his return he told me that the superintendent stated I would not get back. I asked the foreman to get me an interview which was refused, so I decided to take the man who had promised that I would get my work back and see the manager who after phoning the superintendent told him I was to be started. This was years before I had the interview previously mentioned about the promotions. I little knew then that he and I would get to know each other. This getting back again with my seniority was a great victory and I was welcomed back by my mates and especially old T. Boyd who had kept up my union contributions during my absence. I left it every week with a gas worker to pay him.

[*Here McElborough describes a scheme he devised with Boyd to attract young gas workers to join the trade union.* Circa 500 words.]

In the meantime trouble had started in the shipyards [1922]. Shootings and reprisals were a daily occurrence and the military had taken charge of the danger spots in the city. I was taken off the meter work and was told by the superintendent to keep the lamps in Seaforde Street and the Short Strand in repair. This area was one of the dangerous parts for shooting in the city. I asked why I was selected for this position and what had happened to the lamp maintenance man who did this district. I was told that this was a military order to keep this area lit up. I was issued with a permit and was told I would have military protection if I applied to the officer in charge. I had the feeling like Uriah of the Bible I was being sent to the front line.

The people living in this area did not want the street lit as they said they were a target on the streets, and felt more secure from bullets in the dark, but the military who were patrolling this area insisted that the lamps be lit. This was in 1922 and anyone who lived in this area remembers the cross-firing that was kept up day and night. No one would venture out and trams passed this area at full speed empty, or with passengers lying flat on the floor. My first morning with a handcart full of lamps, when the boy who was with me came to the end of the bridge which led into this area he refused to go any further and left me and went back to the workshops. I don't blame the boy, but for the fact that I had a wife and family and was threatened with dismissal if I refused to do this work, I would have given it up.

I can't tell how I got the cart into this area. I ran with it and got safely into Madrid Street and into Seaforde Street with rifles cracking overhead. When I arrived with the lamps and fittings I was surrounded by a number of men and women who told me to clear out. I had to explain my position as a workman. It was the women who carried the day in my favour, but I was told that every lamp and fitting that I fitted up would be smashed when the lights were lit, and I want to say here and now that during these winter months that I kept the lights repaired the people in this area never interfered with me. But there was times when I had to clear out, when someone who lived in the district had been shot by a sniper. It was the snipers on the roofs and back windows who were the danger. Anyone seen on the streets within the range of their gun was their target and they found out later through the press what side he belonged to. I had seen men who were going to work shot dead as a reprisal for some other victim. My only dread was when I was standing on the ladder putting up a lamp. Bullets that I suppose were meant for me went through the lamp reflector. I brought some of these lamps back to the workshops and my workmates had many discussions on my narrow escapes.

My foreman during the time I was engaged in the area never asked me any questions. I got unlimited supplies of lamps and fittings. My superintendent had told me the day that he instructed [me] to do this work he would pay me a visit, but from the first day I started until I was taken off when the clear nights arrived he never put in an appearance. My only visitor during these months was the officer in charge of the military patrol who told me about some lights in other streets that were not burning. These lamps were controlled by the pressure from the gas works. The controller in the lamp had lead weights 10 and 5 and 2½ oz and were supplied with mercury. The bye-pass which was always lit was fitted on the burner and when the pressure was turned on at the works the weights were lifted and the gas entered the fitting and the lit bye-pass did the rest. These controllers were like a scale pressure and in the morning when the pressure was turned off the weights dropped and the lights went out. There was no need for a lamplighter which was a puzzle to the people in the district as they tried to turn the lamps out but could find no tap.

Curfew was in operation.[31] After a certain hour at night everyone had to be indoors. That was one of the reasons I was issued with a permit. The officer had taken my name and address and told me if anything went wrong with the lights during the night he would send a Lancia car to fetch me. But I never was called out. I think it was a disappointment that I came through this unhurt. The tramway committee passed a vote of thanks to the tram-men who drove their trams past this district. I received none. I suppose the officials received all the credit for keeping this area lighted.

We had no branch meetings owing to curfew but no one would have ventured out as the risk was too great. Old T. Boyd had given up the collecting of members' contributions and T. Moore who had returned from the army took over the job. I would like to state that I as an ordinary member of the union was only interested in getting my department a hundred per cent membership. We were making great progress in other municipal departments and we had a strict committee with a member out of each department. We had visits from Peter Levenan[32] and others who brought messages of encouragement from the other side. Our funds were mounting and we had started a sick Section for members and we had assisted a number of poor and distressed members but we had to wait until things got better before having branch meetings.

[*Here McElborough describes the difficulties he had in attracting to the trade union young recruits to the gas industry.* Circa 360 words.]

After the shooting trouble had been a little suppressed the burning of buildings started. I was sent to cut off a number of meters in streets that had been set on fire. One street on the Falls Road was my most dangerous job. A block of six houses were set alight and when the fire brigade fixed their hoses on the water main the snipers cut the hose pipes with their bullets. I was warned by the brigade and the police of the danger I ran with these snipers, but for the danger of the meters exploding I would have backed out but I knew if the fire got a hold of the service pipes in the houses there would be some trouble getting it out. However with the assistance of the Lancia police car, I was able to remove these meters and cap the service pipes. One other meter job at the north end of the city nearly cost me my life. It was an empty shop at the corner of a main road. It was shattered and the rent agent had sent the keys to our office with the request to remove the meter as this shop was in the front line of the snipers and had been hit with bullets a number of times. When I opened the door the shop was in darkness with the shutters being on. When I struck a light, I was confronted by a couple of men with guns. Their faces were covered and I was given a minute to clear out. The boy who was with me disappeared. I asked them to let me cut the meter off but I was told to go and it was only when I got around the corner that I got speed up.

[*Here McElborough describes taking up the case of workers who on Saturday mornings had fallen victim to a manager obsessed with the idea they had spent Friday's wages on alcohol.* Circa 500 words.]

My eldest daughter who had sleepy sickness for 3½ years died and my wife later on followed. My wife who came from a Co. Tyrone family was unlearned about the workers' struggle for wages and conditions but she shared without complaint all my suspensions and victimisations. We had to depend on the generosity of our friends for food during these times and during the 44 hours strike I used to stay away most of the day. I was grateful for the help the friends gave but what was said to me about unions and rebels by these friends when I happened to come in after walking the streets all day was ungrateful. My daughter's death was a great blow to me. I had sent her to friends in Liverpool to see a professor who gave me hope that she might be cured. I don't wish to recall how I got the money to do this but after 6 weeks I was sent word that there was no hope so she came back to die. When she took this dreaded sickness she lost her speech. And to talk to her without a reply was a heartbreak but I know I had to deny her many things during these trying times. I was torn between love and duty. But the picture of my father's and mother's struggle to exist and my determination to better my lot won. My wife died some time after my daughter and I was also down and had been given up by the doctor, but I recovered and my workmates visited me during my illness and kept me informed about trade union affairs. But the MEA had been merged years before [in 1924] with the National Union of Labour. I will refer to this later on. When I returned to work after, I received no word of condolence from any official nor congratulations on my recovery. The rumour that I was dying as some of the workmen said had perhaps given the K.O. to union activities in this department and my return to work was unexpected. There was nothing of importance to record only I was asked to take over the cleaning and maintenance of the City Hall lamps by the foreman. But I declined this as I would have been out of touch with the workers in my department.

The superintendent had decided to retire and there was great activity amongst the favoured to give him a presentation. When I was asked to subscribe to this I was told by the collector that it was the superintendent's wish to have an album with all the employees' names suitably embossed in this album. As I was the 2nd oldest employee I was to be the 2nd in this album. I refused to subscribe as I told the collector my wife and my daughter would turn in their grave if I gave in to this and I would be betraying some of my fellow-members who were dead. His retiring allowance was two-thirds of his salary and I was informed that he made a claim for free gas. As I was not interested in him after he retired I cannot give any information in regard to this. I can claim with pride that I succeeded in enrolling the workers in spite of his hatred of trade unions. He used his position to keep the worker on a low wage but for himself he made applications a few times for an advance in his salary.

[*Here McElborough narrates two stories, one of being sent to install a meter at Crumlin Road Gaol, the other being an example of what he regarded as 'the power of the worker when organised' at Harland & Wolff and of which he heartily approved.* Circa 900 words.]

When the superintendent retired I thought this was a splendid opportunity for me to make an application for this position. It was not advertised and I knew that I stood no chance but I was of the opinion that I had more knowledge of the department than anyone in it, and I had the practical qualifications of heat, light and power. I wrote my application out very carefully giving my service and my age and, before I posted it to the manager, I met a member of the city council who I knew by sight but not to talk to. I stopped him in the street and I told him my intentions. He asked me to read my application, which I did and he told me to post it on to the manager. A week afterwards the vacancy was filled by one of the bosses from the manufacturing section. He was unknown as far as our department was concerned. I must state in fairness to him he respected my knowledge and acted on one occasion on my advice with regard to a gas cooker. He was also sympathetic to any complaints from the members of the union.

[*Here McElborough describes the difficulties encountered by the superintendent's driver when he had been recruited to the trade union.* Circa 400 words.]

Previous to his [the superintendent's] retirement the gas manager had retired and as he was the third gas manager I had worked under and came in contact with him often I would like to give a brief history of him through the eyes of a gas employee, he was appointed to the position at the time when the gas holders in the works was unable to supply the demand for gas. There had been talk about the gas committee wanting a portion of the Ormeau Park to erect a gasholder. The public were up against this proposal, and the new manager when he had looked around the gas works decided against Ormeau Park and received the thanks of the citizens. Not only did he erect a large gas holder in the works, he also done away with the old hand benches but built retort houses that are up to date with any gas undertaking in Britain and before he retired he erected a waterless gas holder which is stated to be the second largest in the gas world. He accomplished this inside the boundary of the gas works. So much for the manufacturing section. The small gas holders which were erected when the late James Stelfox was manager are still in the gas works with his name and the date of their erection.[33] It was Stelfox who was manager when I first started as a boy in the gas department and when he died his place was taken over by Mr Sharp who had been his assistant. Sharp did not reign long until he died and then Mr J. D. Smith was appointed. He made all the above improvements and was able to give 70,000 and sometimes 80,000 [pounds] to the sinking fund of the City Hall, all from gas. With regard to the maintenance and distribution departments, he introduced the Main gas cooker and the Cinderella and the Sunbeam gas fire previous to his appointment. We had three different firms supplying our department with cookers and gas appliances, Fletcher Russell Wright and the Richmond Company. Having a practical knowledge of them all my vote goes to the Main cooker. He also introduced a new type of meter from the Alder & Mackay.

He came from Scotland and he kept his country well to the fore in the Gas Industry. My ancestors also came from Scotland in the 16th century and they settled in Co. Tyrone. Some of them were behind the walls in Derry and others crossed to America and fought on the

American side for Independence. These ancestors of mine were part of the 400,000 protestant Ulstermen and Presbyterians amongst them who helped draw up the declaration of Independence so I am proud to state that I during my career fought on the workers' side for wages and conditions as a descendant of an Ulster Scot.

[*Here McElborough recalls his trade union experiences under this gas manager, including the scheme to recruit junior employees.* Circa 1,000 words.]

All power tends to corruption, Lord Acton states[34]. But this power did not apply to one party only. Union officials who were elected to the council did their share of getting sons, friends and relatives into positions. I know one who even got a corporation house when the corporation were building houses before the 2nd world war. A notice was put up in every department giving employees first preference on these houses, yet this official of the Trade Union used his position and selected the house he intended to live in. And they gull us with the cry that they have no axe to grind. It's at the committee meetings members of the council will tell you that the work is done. I can well believe it. I remember a man whose place of business that he worked in was closing and he questioned me with regard to positions in our department particularly the testing shop as he was a man well up in years. I told him that young men had to learn the meter testing and this work was very important. He asked me regarding other grades, meters, cookers, and lamp maintenance. He seemed rather disappointed for he was picking his position [in] the gas department. He had been promised one, as the owner of the firm which was closing down was a member of the gas committee. What chance has an ordinary workman against this? The manager had his hands tied. He must have the goodwill of his committee otherwise his applications from time to time don't count. It is my contention that the people would get better service if out of the Chamber of Commerce or other bodies who pay large rates 2 or 3 were elected to serve on these committees for the purpose of guarding the ratepayers who could take part in the discussions and vote without fear or favour and 2 workers elected in the works by ballot to look after the workers' side. I believe this would do away with these men who belong to different parties who are only out for what they can get in the way of comfortable positions. This would give the heads of the various departments a free hand to engage the best men and to promote men with ability and qualifications for higher positions. It's the system that has been in operation during my time that I am condemning. I have worked under 3 foremen, 3 superintendents and 4 managers.

To carry on with my story. When the war started in 1939 we had to make a move organising ARP and fire-watching duties.[35] We were instructed to turn out when the sirens sounded and no matter where we were working we must return to the workshops in the daytime. We turned out a number of times but the all-clear went before we reached the workshops, until one night we had the full force of Hitler's might. We had to stand by all night. We were everywhere and it was 6 a.m. before we were told to go home and return again at 8 a.m. and for weeks our work was removing meters from burning buildings. On the third day of this I collapsed and had to be taken home and for 7 weeks I had to remain in bed and every time the sirens went I had to be carried from bed to the back of Broadway football grounds until the all-clear went. Sometimes the sirens alarmed 3 times in the night. For my night's work at the blitz I received the sum of 5/9 and I lost 7 weeks' pay after I returned to work. I had frequent attacks of dizziness and vomiting. The foreman told me that I was exempt from fire-watching and the government committee who sent for me to attend the labour exchange gave me an exemption card. I lost a daughter who was killed by a military car which mounted the pavement and crashed through the shop window which she was looking at whilst shopping. I had been off work again and the doctor advised me not to start. I interviewed the gas manager telling him my National Health insurance had been reduced to 11/– weekly. He told me to come in each day for 2½ hours and I would receive £1 weekly and I would not be required to work. I carried out this until the department sent me to their doctor for a test and an x-ray in the stomach. After this the manager sent for me and told me I was to leave and that I had been granted £1 weekly. I told him that this was a poor reward for a life-time service. He said he had nothing to do with it and he and the assistant manager shook hands with me and told me to watch my health. I know that I am suffering from gas poisoning through working over open service pipes when changing meters and fittings.

[*Here McElborough describes further occupational hazards of fitting meters.* Circa 500 words.]

I will continue my story with my union activities under the Municipal Employees from our branch rooms in May Street for these were the last branch rooms we were to occupy under the old MEA for we were informed in 1924 that we were being merged with the National Union of Labour. This organisation catered for shipyard workers. I remember the late George Gregg who came from Newcastle-on-Tyne.[36] He opened an office in Garfield Street. I had heard him speak on platforms. He died previous to his union being merged with the MEA. This merger to us was a bit of a mystery. As far as our union was concerned our members were in steady and constant employment and our finance was increasing every year. We had started a splendid sick section with different grades and had appointed sick stewards to visit the members who were ill. On the other hand the NUL members who were employed in shipyards were unemployed through the depression and any who remained in the union were only paying 2d [pence] weekly and as our members summed the matter up it was only a question of time until this union went and placed their officials on the street, so they had looked around for an investment for their funds and decided on the MEA. We got no opportunity of voting yes or no and looking back I consider that merger was a fatal mistake not to the officials but to the members. Our official who up to this time had carried out his duties in a faithful manner had came up for re-election every three years, but no-one ever opposed him for his record stood high. I only wish I could say that now. The new branch rooms that were opened in Upper Garfield Street were called by the officials a red-letter day. It certainly was for them. I forget the name of the cross-channel official or star who performed the opening ceremony. I happened to call in the afternoon on my way to work and the officials all seemed very happy. As one of the members remarked it was the mugs money that was making them enjoy themselves. There was what the officials called a reunion in a restaurant to celebrate the merging of the two unions. As I was not interested in boozing parties, I did not attend, but one of our members, A. Moore, who was a member of the district committee attended and gave me full details. The drink flowed like water and a branch official of the shipyard section fell down the stairs and broke his neck and died. It was a bad beginning. This man was employed in the shipyard foundry and lived convenient to me.

[*Here McElborough describes the circumstances of his union joining the NUGMW. Circa 500 words.*]

Our new title was the National Union of General and Municipal Workers and we were affiliated to the Trades Union congress, the Labour Party, Confederation of Engineering and Shipbuilding Unions, National Federation of Building Trades Operatives and Municipal and Public Service Workers International, and Factory Workers International.[37] When we inquired if we had to contribute to all these we were told that by supporting these affiliations we had them supporting us in the event of a strike. We began to wonder how we had won all our victories up to now without these. What Will Thorne thought about it, when he was placed in an advisory capacity is, I suppose, unknown but he received a good salary when he handed over the reins of what he had founded. Charley Dukes[38], his successor, like myself was a member of the MEA but his history bears no comparison with Will Thorne. I interviewed him on one occasion but the brotherly spirit of Will Thorne was absent. Perhaps he thought I was carrying a revolver but looking around his office before he arrived I could not help but contrast it with the old office of Will Thorne in Tavistock Square. He took over a fine mansion in Rusholme, Manchester and named it Thorne House, when he was a district official in that area and now he is boss of the head office in Endsleigh Gardens.

[*Here McElborough rails against those responsible for the amalgamation, particularly Charles Dukes.* Circa 2000 words.]

Our organiser had got bitten by a bug and he stood as a candidate for Cromac ward for the city council [1920] but he made a poor show and we had to organise a ballot to clear his expenses. His complaint at our branch meetings was that he could not get into the council committees as he was not a member and he had to await the result of claims and grievances of members outside the committee rooms. So we decided we would put him forward for St George's ward in the city council.[39] If it were possible to see into the future or to judge men it would alter your movements to a large extent. St George's ward is the ward that I was bred and born in. It is the smallest municipal ward in the city. It consists of two main roads, Donegall Road and famous Sandy Row. It is an industrial district with working-class houses on each of these main roads. Our old organiser Alex Boyd won it for labour when he was secretary of the MEA. He was defeated at the next election for the part he took in the dockers' side during the strike, but he was successful later on when he stood for Alderman as independent Labour. He had given up as a union organiser at this election. I took prominent part in these elections on Boyd's side but when Alderman Boyd died undergoing an operation the municipal workers lost a great friend, especially the gas workers for he had been a stoker in the gas works and his practical experience of vertical work commanded respect from the gas manager at committee meetings.

So when a number of members talked the matter over we decided to put our organiser up for this ward. The opposition candidate was Col. B. Browne who later on became MP for West Belfast in the Imperial parliament.[40] He was a gentleman who was interested in social work amongst the cripples and had an institute in this way for these people and he was very popular amongst the people for his good work. It is an election that I will always remember. I was known to the majority of the people and I went into the midst of the people who lived around this institute to canvass on behalf of our organiser. I want to state that if there are parts of your life that you wished to forget,

especially the poverty part in your young life you will be reminded
about them by old people, women in particular, who can tell you when
and where you were born and remind you about your petticoat stage.
These old women received gifts of tea and cake at Xmas time and were
invited to parties occasionally in this institute. My companion during
the canvassing of this election was Andrew Moore, our district delegate, and many a laugh we had afterwards when we recalled the night
we were chased by women with brushes. Our union official was elected
with a majority of 7.

[*Here McElborough describes the 'great mistake' they made in electing this councillor who developed a 'superiority complex'.* Circa 500 words.]

It was Moore that gave me the information that we were to be
merged with Liverpool. I was unaware that I as branch secretary
should have received the minutes of the executive and general council
from our district official. It would have given me information with
regard to the re-organisation business. Nor did I ever receive the half-
yearly financial return which is issued from head office and is passed
on to branch secretaries of the union. Moore as our district delegate
told us the news at our branch meeting and our organiser also. This
news was a shock to us as our membership had been increasing and the
loss of our district was something we could not comprehend. The district Secretary was to retire on a pension and the district office was to
be in Liverpool and Belfast was to be an area office or as some of the
members stated a rubber stamp office. We unfortunately received this
information too late to take any action in the way of a protest. So all
we could do was to await events. There is not any doubt whatever that
the Irish members were opposed to this change and if they had been
given the opportunity to vote on this they would have rejected it.
Members of other branches who met you were up in arms but had no
redress. All our past history as pioneers of Trade Unionism had been
wiped out without a protest from the representative who attended
these meetings.

[*Here McElborough provides considerable detail on the effects of the merger and also describes his own unsuccessful attempts to get elected.* Circa 10,000 words.]

To give an idea of the work as I and collecting stewards carried out each week-end. The collecting stewards in the gas works collected the contributions on pay night inside the works. When I took over the duties of branch secretary, to keep myself right with the management, I got permission to visit the gas works, as I was employed as an outdoor maintenance man. Our department was across the street from the works. I finished work as an outdoor man at 5 every evening and the inside workers finished at 5.30. That included the gas works and when I finished work on pay day I crossed over to the works and met the collecting stewards. From that and until the buzzer sounded I was busy dealing with complaints or receiving medical certificates and contribution cards from the collecting stewards and getting a number of old age pensioners forms to fill in. When the buzzer sounded there would be a rush by the workers to get their wages and the two collecting stewards were up to the neck taking and marking members contributions and when the workers had told me a number of complaints or had asked me regarding their rate of wages or told me about being paid short on overtime, you had to receive the contributions from the stewards, count it and give them a receipt and sometimes you were successful in getting the workers whose wages were short fixed up for the following week through the time-keeper, and sometimes you had a death claim and you had to visit the member's home to get the death certificate after you had your tea. Our union always inserted in the newspaper a member's death until Liverpool took charge when we were told to stop these insertions on the plea of expense. It was 6.30 when I got clear of the gas works every Friday.

I had no need to do this it could be said. I always said that personal attendance every week gave the members a chance to tell you their complaints. It would have surprised the union officials if they had been interested in the members to know how difficulties were smoothed over. Members who were in the National Health section would have asked you to get them forms for optical and dental complaints. You were engaged over the weekend at home doing this business. I carried out this weekly visit to the gas works during the years I was branch secretary and I loved the work. To me it was very interesting and I attribute this to the large and contented membership. I did not know then but I know now how loyal they were to be when the occasion demanded it. Many Fridays during the winters when I was wet through after working outdoor all day I had to stand in a draughty entry where the workers were paid in the gas works carrying out this work. The most difficult time was during the war in the winter evenings. I carried a torch to show the collecting stewards their book to mark the members' contributions. There was no light owing to the black outs. I could not draw a picture but many times when the collecting stewards and I were taking what shelter we could find whilst waiting for the horn to blow I have pictured in my imagination the union officials in their offices with their gas fires and their telephones and their cars, whilst we were bringing in the dough to keep these men and then to read in this book about the generous manner in which they were paid. If it were not for the branch officials they would not be living in good homes with baths in the suburbs, starting off to business with clerical workers and in receipt of good salaries and pensions when they retire.

[*Here McElborough describes union politicking on the question of a change of hours for shift workers.* Circa 1,300 words.]

It was some time previous to this that my daughter whilst shopping had been killed by a military lorry which had mounted the pavement and crashed into a shop window pinning her beneath it. I had been stopping in her home and when her husband had given me the news of her death, it about finished me as I had been off ill and was making no progress.

I had been looking for a house as I did not wish to be a burden on her, so I had decided, if I got a house, to get married. I had got word of a small shop with a house attached that the owner was giving up as his wife had died after one of the blitz[es]. I interviewed this man who insisted that the house and shop must go together. I had to take it and he said he could make a living in the shop. I told him my health was gone and he promised he would show my wife how to take charge. I had to give this business up when I was able to obtain a smaller house. I had to engage qualified persons and paid them a good wage but on my final reckoning I was on the losing side. I have nothing to complain about only that neither my wife nor I qualified. This shop would give a man and his wife a good living if they took control, but my income during this period was 11/– weekly disablement and my total loss was £168, so I had to give it up or go to the workhouse if I had stayed on.

The death of my daughter was a heavy blow and to make it worse I had to attend the hospital to identify her. The memory of what I looked at when the doctor pulled the sheet down will always remain with me. The doctor told me that her body was all smashed up and her brain had been damaged with the radiator in front of the car. I was in a sort of a daze for weeks after it and it was the companionship of my wife that kept me from thinking over it.

I had decided to resign from the secretary of the local sick section that I had founded in opposition to the one the district secretary had taken from us without our permission, so when I was told that I was unfit for work in June 1942 and told some of the committee my intentions they asked me to try and carry on until the annual meeting in January 1943. When I handed over this local sick section, I handed over two bank books containing £165. Not bad going in four years after paying out hundreds of pounds in sickness benefit and death claims. Our weekly contributions were 4d, a penny a week less than the Liverpool section. I was very proud of this local sick, proud because I was told by union officials that three months would end it and I was pleased by the tributes that were paid to me by those best able to judge the members. My experience in another friendly society, the Shepherds, as secretary, helped me to separate the wheat from the chaff and the assistance of a good committee. I was really sorry that I had to give it up for it was visiting the sick members in their homes and talking to them that was the interesting part of my duties.

I had at this time been receiving £1 weekly that the administrators had granted me. The gas manager had sent for me and told me that I had been given this £1 weekly. He said he was sorry at losing my services after all these years and he advised me to take care of myself. He and the assistant manager shook hands with me and that was the finish of my career in the gas Industry in which I had given a lifetime service. I was at this time almost 60, and I had started in this industry as a boy at 14. I had no intention of taking this dismissal without doing something about it. My union was out of the question after what had happened so I interviewed a gentleman who is connected with a deaf institute. He was interested in me when I had on a previous visit wanted information on lip reading. I had told him my defective hearing was due to the chemical in the gas when working over open service pipes whilst changing gas meters. I gave him a report on the class of work I had been engaged on, and I told him I had been sent by the gas department to be examined and x-rayed and I had been told I was finished. After taking these statements, he told me he would see one of the administrators and told me to come back again and he would let me know the result. When I visited him again he told [me] that I would be looked after. I asked him how as I was only receiving National Health disablement of 11/– weekly. I next visited my Health Insurance Society and after stating my case I was told that this society had no solicitor to fight claims for compensation, and if I took this case to the law courts they would have to stop my health insurance benefit until I had got the verdict. My next visit was to the member of parliament for South Belfast, Lieut Col. H. Gage[41], who gave me a sympathetic hearing. He promised to see Mr Lindgrin, parliamentary secretary to the Minister of the National Health Insurance.[42] During this interview I put forward a suggestion with regard to payments under the present Health Insurance system, where people who were insured, when ill, if they went to the country or the seaside had to pay train or bus fares into the city to see their doctor and to receive their medical certificate, and I pointed out that this could be paid to these people through the post and the doctor could on his first medical line state the period which a sick person would be off ill. My experience during the years I had been secretary and listening to the complaints was that this was a genuine grievance. Wives of members, when visiting these members to pay their sick claims, would tell you that they would take their husbands to the country or the seaside to help them only for the visit to the doctor each week. My sympathy was with these complaints so the social security bill was a fine opportunity to put forward this suggestion. Mr H. C. Gage and I had some correspondence with regard to my case for compensation and he told me that I could put up my claim for compensation under the Industrial Injuries Bill which was part of the new National Health Insurance Bill.

It was sometime later [ca. 1945] that I received a letter from Mr Gage congratulating me on having made a contribution to the law of the country. 'It is not', he states, 'everyone who can say that. I am enclosing a letter from Mr Lindgrin, Parliamentary Secretary to the Ministry of National Insurance. From it you will see that it has been decided to incorporate your suggestion into the new scheme'. The enclosed letter which contains my suggestion ends up with, in ink, 'Thanks so much for your interest and helpful suggestions, any more which come to you, please do pass them on to us'. This was published in one of the local newspapers the following morning under the title 'An Ulsterman with an Ulster plan' and gave the details.

[*Here McElborough describes disputes surrounding the proposed transfer of Belfast tramways and bus employees from his union to the Ulster Transport & Allied Operatives Union.* Circa 1900 words.]

The gas workers all over had been fighting for a sick pay scheme. I had met gas workers on the other side of the channel and I had letters from others on this matter for to me gas was a universal language. Whenever I crossed to England when I saw a gas holder, I was sure to meet my fellow gas worker and compare notes on wages and conditions. I got some surprises when getting his information. To visit a union office was to know in advance what you would be told. I got handed to me in one of these offices agreements that gave me no information on what I was seeking. So that is why I like to talk to the worker on these matters and that is why these reports from these officials are all self-praise. This bill had no effect on the gas workers who had joined the new union but at this period the members of the new union decided to apply to the open council meeting of the corporation. This application would embrace all municipal works, as workers from the non-trading departments were joining this new union. This application for recognition which came before the full council meeting received 25 votes against 9. This was considered a great victory for the members who had received many hard knocks during this battle, but had delivered the knock-out in the final round. As some of the gas workers expressed it they had shaken off their chains and were free to control their own affairs. I am sure if Moore had been alive he would have been pleased for he said when we were merged to Liverpool that all our years of building had been swept away. There is little more to be told only that the union official announced his retirement owing to ill-health. He was the last of the merger officials. He had a long innings. He used to tell me after a branch meeting when he made tracks for his public house that he owned shares in it and I would tell him in reply that he should change the name to the union bar. If the tables the officials sat at could speak they could tell some tales. . .

Well, I have come to the end of my story and I have fulfilled my promise to my dead colleague Brother Andrew Moore. About my own advice to the gas workers, I would say: Form your own union on the same lines as the miners, appoint your own delegates and finally look after your old veterans and don't throw them on the scrap heap. It is not given to everyone to have their own funeral claim and to be alive to read it but as the late Lord Dwyer used to say in his after-dinner speeches, when a doctor makes a mistake it's buried. But my union can't bury their mistake. At least, I hope not, now that I have written my story of 40 years in the Trade Union movement. The union officials might wish to treat me as a forgotten factor, but my workmates don't and they are the best judge of one who fought their battles.

Abbreviations

ATGWU	Amalgamated Transport and General Workers' Union
IOO	Independent Orange Order
MEA	Municipal Employees' Association
NAUL	National Amalgamated Union of Labour
NUGMW	National Union of General and Municipal Workers
NUGW	National Union of General Workers
NIC/ITUC	Northern Ireland Committee of the Irish Trade Union Congress
PRONI	Public Record Office of Northern Ireland
TUC	Trades Union Congress
UTAOU	Ulster Transport and Allied Operatives' Union

Notes to Introduction

1. The Civil Registration of Births records the birth on 11 February 1884 of 'Robert Henry McEllborough' (not 'McElborough'). PRONI, MIC/165/14, vol 1 p. 220.

2. 'Of the ten largest cities in the United Kingdom, none grew more rapidly than Belfast over the period 1841–1901.' A. C. Hepburn, 'Work, class and religion in Belfast, 1871–1911', *Irish Economic and Social History,* x (1983), p. 33.

3. 1952 Wills and Letters of Administration Index, p. 278, records the death on 29 March 1952 of Robert Henry McElborough 'retired cooker repairer', the effects to 'Margaret Lindsay McElborough, the widow', PRONI.

4. See *Report of the Deputy Keeper of the Records, 1954–9,* p. 97 which records the deposit of '4 vols. Diaries kept by Robert McElborough, Coolfin Street, in which he comments on "my years in the gas industry and my fight with the trade unions".' The diaries are numbered D/770/1/1–4, the correspondence D/770/2/1–11.

5. Made available as *An Autobiography of a Belfast Working Man* (Belfast, 1974).

6. Discrimination in municipal employment, where McElborough spent most of his working life, was virtually 'quantifiable'. In the 1900s, when Catholics formed about 25% of the population of Belfast, they held 28% of central government jobs, and 9% of local government jobs in the city. Hepburn, 'Work, class and religion in Belfast, 1871–1911', p. 50.

7. See J. W. Boyle, 'The Belfast Protestant Association and the Independent Orange Order, 1901–10', *Irish Historical Studies,* xiii, no. 50 (1962), pp. 117–52; and Austen Morgan, *Labour and Partition: The Belfast Working Class, 1905–23* (London, 1991), pp. 43–59.

8. *Northern Whig*, 19 Jan. 1910, quoted in Morgan, *Labour and Partition,* p. 51.

9. Henry Patterson, *Class Conflict and Sectarianism: The Protestant Working Class and the Belfast Labour Movement, 1868–1920* (Belfast, 1980), p. 134; Alec Wilson, *PR: Urban Elections in Ulster, 1920* (London, 1972), pp. 16, 28–29.

10. Peter Gerard Collins, 'Belfast trades council, 1881–1921' (D. Phil, University of Ulster, 1988), appendix 3. Details on the MEA in Belfast are sparse, but see John W. Boyle, *The Irish Labor Movement in the Nineteenth Century* (Washington DC, 1988), pp. 166, 286; Morgan, *Labour and Partition*; and Patterson, *Class Conflict and Sectarianism*. The official history of the MEA/NUGMW is H. A. Clegg, *General Union in a Changing Society: A Short History of the National Union of General and Municipal Workers, 1889–1964* (Oxford, 1964).

11. Like Boyd, Bowman had the advantage of being a city councillor. See Terence Bowman, *People's Champion: The Life of Alexander Bowman, Pioneer of Labour Politics in Ireland* (Belfast, 1997), pp. 121–56.

12. A fine study is John Gray, *City in Revolt: James Larkin and the Belfast Dock Strike of 1907* (Belfast, 1985).

13. Gray, *City in Revolt*, pp. 191–203.

14. Gray, *City in Revolt*, p. 238.

15. Houston was active on Belfast trades' council, became an organiser for the Irish Transport and General Workers' Union in Oct. 1916, was based in Cork initially but transferred to Belfast in 1918, and was elected to Belfast Corporation as a Labour councillor in 1920. See C. Desmond Greaves, *The Irish Transport and General Workers' Union: The Formative Years, 1909–23* (Dublin, 1982).

16. Ministry of Labour reports on strikes and lockouts, 1918, LAB 34/36, Public Record Office, London.

17. Morgan, *Labour and Partition*, pp. 229–49.

18. Morgan, *Labour and Partition*, pp. 265, 270.

19. Collins, 'Belfast trades council, 1881–1921', p. 299; Patterson, *Class Conflict and Sectarianism*, p. 134; Morgan, *Labour and Partition*, pp. 273–4.

20. G. B. McKenna, *Facts and Figures: The Belfast Pogroms, 1920–22* (Dublin, 1997 reprint), p. 101.

21. Ken Coates and Tony Topham, *The History of the Transport and General Workers' Union*, I, part 2 (Oxford, 1991), p. 861. The NUGMW later became the General, Municipal, Boilermakers and Allied Trades Union, and in 1989 the GMB.

22. Thorne (1857–1946) served on the TUC Parliamentary Committee [executive], 1894–1934, and was an MP, 1906–45. See also Will Thorne, *My Life's Battles* (London, 1927).

23. Boyle, *The Irish Labor Movement*, p. 111.

24. Thorne, *My Life's Battles*, pp. 158–9.

25. Thorne, *My Life's Battles*, p. 47.

26. Hugh Armstrong Clegg, *A History of British Trade Unions Since 1889*, ii (Oxford, 1985), p. 109.

27. Clegg, *A History of British Trade Unions*, pp. 201–2; Coates and Topham, *The History of the Transport and General Workers' Union*, p. 773.

28. Clegg, *General Union in a Changing Society*, pp. 62, 103.

29. Clegg, *A History of British Trade Unions*, p. 350.

30. Clegg, *A History of British Trade Unions*, pp. 350–1; Tony Lane, *The Union Makes Us Strong: The British Working Class, Its Trade Unionism and Politics* (London, 1974), p. 236.

31. Henry Pelling, *A History of British Trade Unionism* (Harmondsworth, 1974), p. 205. Dukes (1881–1948) remained NUGMW General Secretary until 1946.

32. Clegg, *General Union in a Changing Society*, pp. 109, 139–40, 211.

33. PRONI, D/770/1/4, ff. 31–7.

34. Emmet O'Connor, *A Labour History of Ireland, 1824–1960* (Dublin, 1992), pp. 188, 193; Terence Gerard Cradden, 'Trade unionism and socialism in Northern

Ireland, 1939–53' (PhD thesis, Queen's University, Belfast, 1988), pp. 432–33; Terry Cradden, *Trade Unionism, Socialism, and Partition: The Labour Movement in Northern Ireland, 1939–53* (Belfast, 1993), pp. 142, 165.

Notes to Narrative

1. In 1949, McElborough gave the diaries to John Hewitt, Curator of Art in the Belfast Museum & Art Gallery, who in July 1956 deposited them in the Public Record Office of Northern Ireland, where they may be consulted as D/770/1/1–4. The editors are grateful to Dr David Lammey and Mr J. C. Nolan for their help in verifying this information.

2. Andrew Nance, manager, Belfast Street Tramway Co., who lived at Beechmount, Derryvolgie Avenue, originally the home of R. J. McConnell, the auctioneer and property developer.

3. The 1901 Census Enumerator's return for 35 Coolbeg St lists the names of four McElborough children, all boys, offspring of William and Margaret: William, then aged 20, Robert 17, Henry 15 and John 8. PRONI, MIC/354/1/84.

4. The Education Act, 1892 introduced a limited school attendance requirement in Ireland, following compulsory education legislation in England in 1880. 'Parents in cities and urban areas . . . were required to send children between the ages of 6 and 14 to school for at least 75 days a year.' See Áine Hyland and Kenneth Milne (eds), *Irish Educational Documents*, i (Dublin, 1987), p. 136.

5. 'Half-time' pupils attended school three days in one week and the mill the other two days; the following week, they worked in the mill for three days and went to school for two.

6. Pouce was flax-dust which affected the lungs, particularly of workers in the hackling room. The tow was the broken fibres of the flax being prepared for spinning. Together they created an atmosphere which congested lungs. See Betty Messenger, *Picking Up the Linen Threads: A Study in Industrial Folklore* (Belfast 1975), pp. 98–100.

7. The Theatre Royal in Arthur Square, which became the Royal Cinema in 1914.

8. James Doran, Unionist, represented St Anne's on Belfast Corporation.

9. Sparemen were reserve staff who would stand in for an absentee.

10. Thomas Gallaher, founder of Gallaher Ltd, tobacco manufacturers, York Street, from 1867, having begun in Londonderry in 1857.

11. The statue of Rev. Dr Henry Cooke in College Square, a well-known city-centre landmark more usually referred to as 'the Black Man'.

12. McElborough rejoined the Gas Dept in 1913, but is probably referring here to

Easter Tuesday, 9 April 1912, when 300,000 people took part in a demonstration at the Balmoral Showgrounds, organized by the Orange Order and the Ulster Unionist Council's recently formed Unionist Clubs.

13. Castle Junction, the principal tram centre in Belfast.

14. James Craig, Unionist, represented Cromac on Belfast Corporation.

15. Terence Bowman believes Alexander Bowman ended all involvement with trade unionism on taking a post as superintendent of the Corporation's Falls Road baths in 1901. See Terence Bowman, *People's Champion: The Life of Alexander Bowman, Pioneer of Labour Politics in Ireland* (Belfast, 1997), pp. 157–66.

16. The retort house was where the coal was heated in the process of manufacturing gas.

17. The Central Hall was attached to the Rosemary Street Non-Subscribing Presbyterian Church, well known for its generally liberal tendencies.

18. The *Ulster Guardian* was edited by Robert Lindsay Crawford, Grand Master of the Independent Orange Order. First published in 1903, it finally closed in the 1920s.

19. The sequence here is confusing. Campbell-Bannerman formed a Liberal government in 1905, was re-elected in 1906, and was succeeded by Asquith as Prime Minister in 1908. The Liberals moved to the left under Asquith and, in particular, Lloyd George as Chancellor of the Exchequer, who introduced a reform budget in 1909. The National Insurance Act, which provided state health and unemployment insurance schemes for workers, became law in 1911.

20. A socialist agitator in the 1880s, John Burns (1858–1943) was unofficial leader of the Lib–Lab MPs from 1895, and President of the Local Government Board in the Liberal government, 1906–14.

21. Thomas Burt (1837–1922) was secretary of the Northumberland Miners' Association, 1865–1905, and a Liberal MP, 1874–1918.

22. Joseph Arch (1826–1919) was founder and President of the National Agricultural Labourers' Union, 1873–87; and a Liberal MP, 1885–86, and 1892–1900.

23. Samuel Young was a Nationalist MP for East Cavan, 1892–1918.

24. R. G. Glendinning was an Independent Unionist and 'Russellite' MP for North Antrim, 1906–10.

25. William A. Redmond (1886–1932), eldest son of John Redmond, was a Nationalist MP for East Tyrone, 1910–18.

26. The fourth Earl Dunraven (1841–1926) was associated with a modest devolution proposal for Ireland and 'constructive Unionism'.

27. Fr Patrick Convery, parish priest of St Paul's, Belfast, a native of Maghera, Co. Londonderry and a strong Parnellite, was President of the Belfast Branch of the National League. See D. Curran, *The Story of St Paul's, Belfast* (Belfast, 1987), p. 68.

28. To evade the proscription of a St Patrick's Day meeting, de Valera opened the proceedings at 11 pm on 16 March, with, as McElborough recalls, a truculent

speech. The police drew batons at midnight. See Tim Pat Coogan, *De Valera: Long Fellow, Long Shadow* (London, 1993), p. 103. Sean MacEntee and Dr Russell McNabb were leading Belfast Sinn Feiners. MacEntee later served in every Fianna Fail government from 1932 to 1965.

29. The artist William Conor (1881–1968), who deliberately dropped one of the 'n's in his family name.

30. Arthur Trew, founder of the Belfast Protestant Association, was one of the most regular contributors to Sunday evening orations from the steps of the Custom House, Belfast's Hyde Park Corner.

31. A curfew was introduced in Belfast on 13 May 1922, effective between 9 p.m. and 7 a.m.

32. Probably Peter Tevenen, MEA Organizer and District Secretary, 1905–13, and General Secretary, 1913–24; and NUGMW Assistant General Secretary, 1924–33.

33. James Stelfox jnr, Manager of Belfast Gasworks, 1875–1907. His father had been manager before him, 1852–75.

34. A reference to the adage 'Power tends to corrupt and absolute power corrupts absolutely', first coined by Lord Acton (1834–1907) in a letter to Bishop Mandell Creighton, 3 Apr. 1887. See *The Life and Letters of Mandell Creighton* (1904), i, p. 372.

35. Air Raid Precautions. There were four wartime air raids on Belfast, all in 1941, on the nights of 7–8 and 15–16 April, and 4–6 May, in which at least 889 people were killed, 745 of them in the 'Easter Tuesday' bombing of 15–16 April. The city continued to suffer false alarms over the next two years. For Belfast's unpreparedness and the shock of the Blitz see John W. Blake, *Northern Ireland in the Second World War* (Belfast, 1956), and Brian Barton, *The Blitz: Belfast in the War Years* (Belfast, 1989).

36. Probably George Greig, a longtime NAUL official in Belfast. He died in 1919.

37. The reference to the Factory Workers' International is unclear.

38. Here again McElborough conflates the Gasworkers' Union and the MEA. Dukes had been a Branch and District Secretary of the Gasworkers'/National Union of General Workers, 1911–24. A radical in his early years, Dukes opposed World War I and was imprisoned as a conscientious objector on the adoption of conscription in Britain in 1916.

39. The NAUL fielded three candidates in the 1920 municipal elections: James Johnston in Pottinger, A. Lockett in Victoria, and Sam Bradley in Woodvale. None were elected. Bradley became Irish District Secretary, NUGMW, 1924–37, and was a councillor for Woodvale, 1924–25.

40. Probably Captain A. C. Browne, councillor for St George's, 1925–27, and Unionist MP at Westminster for West Belfast from 1931 until his death in 1942.

41. Lt-Colonel Hugh Conolly Gage was Unionist MP at Westminster for South Belfast from 1945 until his resignation in 1952.

42. George Lindgren, MP, was Parliamentary Secretary to the Ministry of National Health Insurance from August 1945 to October 1946.

Bibliography

Bardon, Jonathan, *Belfast: A Century* (Belfast, 2000)

Beckett, J.C. and Glasscock, R.E. (eds), *Belfast: The Origins and Growth of an Industrial City* (London, 1967)

Boyle, J.W., 'The Belfast Protestant Association and the Independent Orange Order, 1901–10', *Irish Historical Studies*, xiii, no.50 (1962), pp.117–52

Clegg, H. A., *General Union in a Changing Society: A Short History of the National Union of General and Municipal Workers, 1889–1964* (Oxford, 1964)

Coates, Ken and Topham, Tony, *The History of the Transport and General Workers' Union*, i, part II (Oxford, 1991)

Cradden, Terry, *Trade Unionism, Socialism, and Partition: The Labour Movement in Northern Ireland, 1939–53* (Belfast, 1993)

Gray, John, *City in Revolt: James Larkin and the Belfast Dock Strike of 1907* (Belfast, 1985)

Greaves, C. Desmond, *The Irish Transport and General Workers' Union: The Formative Years, 1909–23* (Dublin, 1982)

Morgan, Austen, *Labour and Partition: The Belfast Working Class, 1905–23* (London, 1991)

Patterson, Henry, *Class Conflict and Sectarianism: The Protestant Working Class and the Belfast Labour Movement, 1868–1920* (Belfast, 1980)

Thorne, Will, *My Life's Battles* (London, 1927)

Index